# ...we could live sustainably – by design?

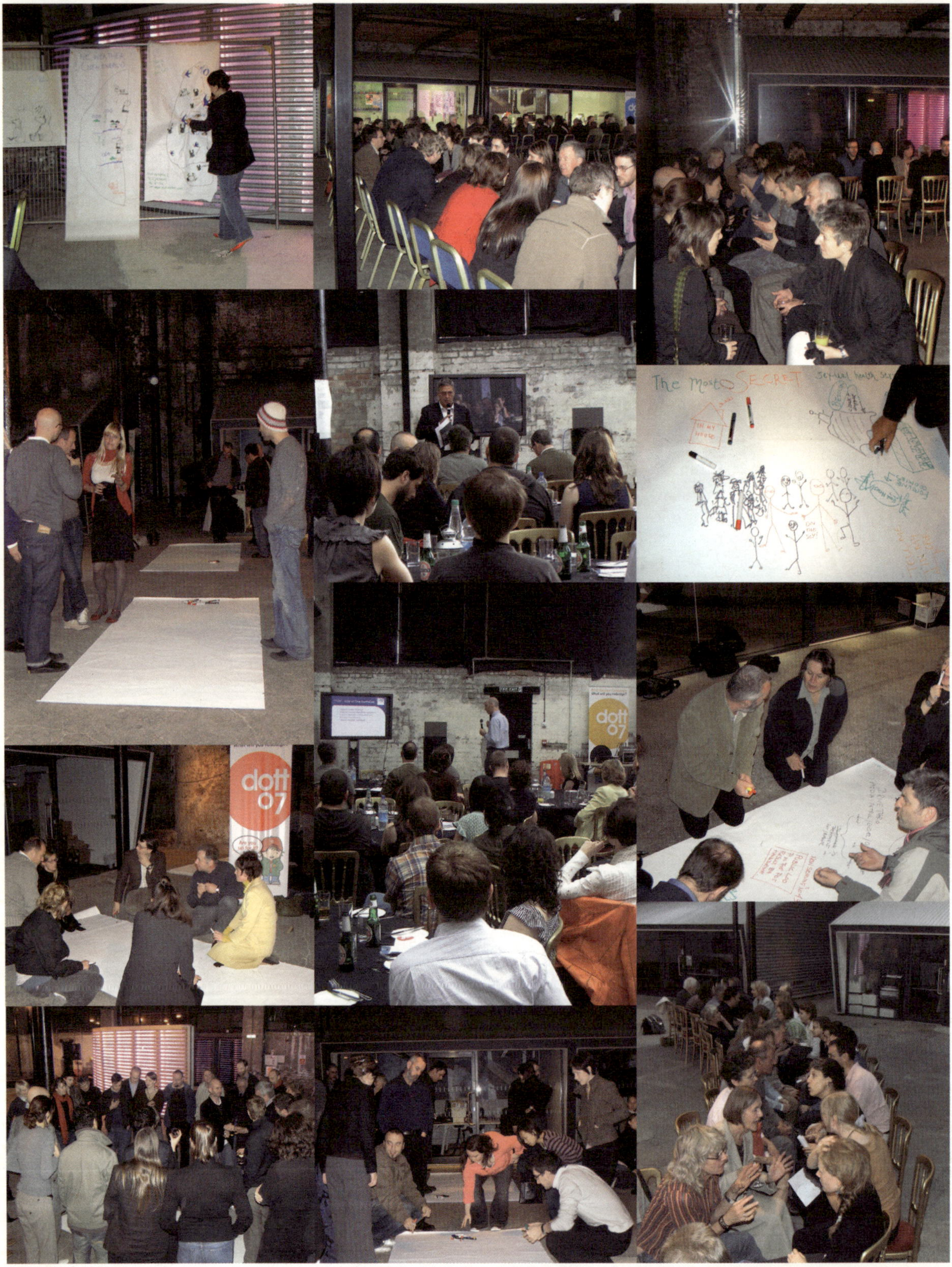
The Most SECRET
dott 07
dott 07

# Better lives with less stuff?

Dott 07 (Designs of the time 2007), a year of community projects, events and exhibitions based in North East England, explored what life in a sustainable region could be like – and how design can help us get there.

A national initiative of the Design Council with the regional development agency One NorthEast, Dott 07 is the first in a 10-year programme of biennial events developed by the Design Council that will take place across the UK. The projects were small but important real-life examples of sustainable living, which will evolve and multiply in the years ahead.

Several projects were delivered in partnership with Culture[10], based at NewcastleGateshead Initiative. Culture[10] manages North East England's world-class festival and events programme.

The projects aim to improve five aspects of daily life: movement, energy, school, health and food.

The focus of the initiative was on grassroots community projects, but there were also projects involving more than 70 schools, plus exhibitions and events in museums, galleries and rural sites. All events explored how design can improve our lives in meaningful ways.

Throughout the Dott year, enthusiastic citizens met with designers, policy makers and subject experts at monthly Explorers' Clubs. The year culminated in a free 12-day Dott 07 Festival in Baltic Square on the banks of the River Tyne. It brought together the results of the projects and enabled all those involved to share their experiences and plan what to do next. Outstanding achievements were celebrated with Creative Community Awards.

Above all, the festival was an opportunity for many more people to find out how to participate in similar projects – and thereby accelerate the region's transition to one planet living.

The Dott 07 Festival was divided into the following zones, which are reflected in this manual:

- **MOVEMENT**
- **ENERGY**
- **SCHOOLS**
- **HEALTH**
- **FOOD**

An additional section at the start of the manual, titled Vital Signs, introduces a series of Dott 07 projects that explored how we measure sustainability. Finally, pages 88 to 95 give details of other project work that has been running alongside Dott 07 throughout the past year.

**Opposite:** at Dott's monthly Explorer's Club, a wide mix of people from the region met in speed meetings, heard from one planet living experts and did rapid-fire design exercises. The ideas that emerged were fed instantly back into Dott projects on the ground

## A new industrial revolution

When North East-born George Stephenson designed his steam locomotive *Rocket* in 1829, he helped set in motion an industrial revolution that transformed everyday life for millions of people around the world. Since then, designers and industry have filled the world with an amazing array of products and buildings, transport and communication networks.

Many of these innovations had unexpected consequences – not all of them good ones. The parlous condition of the planet – our only home – is a good example. The industrial revolution gave us miraculous products, but we produced them in wasteful and polluting ways – and still do.

The benefits of new technology once seemed obvious: better, faster, smarter (and usually cheaper) products. But pointless gadgets and over-complicated devices no longer excite us. And one of the consequences of a technology-filled 'self-service' economy is reduced social contact between people in their everyday lives.

Consumer society no longer makes us happy, if it ever did.

## What's this got to do with design?

Eighty per cent of the environmental impact of today's products, services and infrastructures is determined at the design stage. Design decisions shape the processes behind the products we use, the materials and energy required to make them, the ways we operate them and what happens to them when we no longer need them.

The UK economy has doubled in size since the 1970s; British design and creativity have played an important role in that success. But our satisfaction with life has not kept pace with economic growth. The idea that to be better off we must consume more no longer holds true. The same paradox applies to public services. Our expectations have grown and our spending has increased – but we are frustrated that not all our demands are being met.

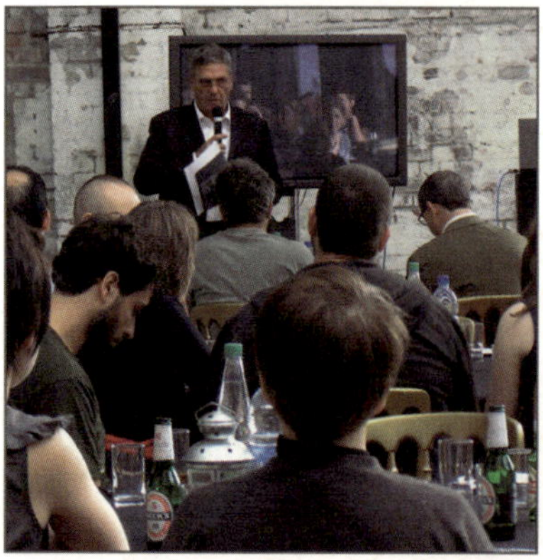

Dott 07 Programme Director John Thackara leads an Explorer Club event

*"North East England has already proven its commitment to using design to create a more dynamic regional economy. Leading the way with a series of bold and innovative initiatives in business, technology and education, the region's plans for long-term investment and thriving cultural programmes make it the ideal choice to host the very first national design promotion – the very first Dott in 2007".*

David Kester, Chief Executive of the Design Council

## How you can build on what Dott has started

Dott 07 explored ways in which we can carry out familiar, daily-life activities in new ways. It is a step towards a 'less stuff, more people' world in which new services will help us share the load of everyday activities: washing clothes, looking after children, communal kitchens and gardens, communal workshops for maintenance activities, tool and equipment sharing, networks and clubs for healthcare and prevention.

Many of these services will involve using products to carry them out but, as a rule, products play a supporting role as a means to an end, and new principles (above all, sustainability and one planet living) inform the ways they are designed, made, used and looked after.

## Why the North East?

The dream of Dott 07 is that the whole North East region will become a kind of design school in which a wide variety of people – not just professionals – meet, share ideas, discuss and learn from each other's experiences.

Dott 07 was not about telling people in the North East how to live. On the contrary: its purpose was to enable local people – interacting with inspiring and visionary guests from around the world – to develop their own visions and scenarios.

In that sense, Dott 07 was in the acorn business. Its most valuable legacy will be the people who remain in the region, the projects they started and the skills they have acquired to carry them out.

The North East will once again be the birthplace of an industrial revolution – only this time it will be sustainable, include a lot of public sector innovation, and draw on the traditions of social solidarity that make the region so special.

## What happens after Dott 07?

The Dott biennial will move from region to region all over the UK over the next eight years.

Dott 07 in North East England has been a one-year-only event, but the idea has been to get things moving on several different fronts.

At the end of each project in this manual, a 'What next?' section tells you what plans are afoot for the project in question. We also suggest books, websites and organisations that you can go to for more information.

# Vital Signs: when would our region be sustainable?

How will we know when our region is 'sustainable'? And how do we get from here, to there? The answers to these questions vary wildly. Vague promises to use "as few natural resources as possible", "reduce waste to a minimum" or deliver the "greenest Olympics planned so far" don't mean very much. As a target, 'increasingly sustainable' is a cop-out. We need to know how much things need to change, and by when.

Four Dott 07 projects, grouped together as Vital Signs, approached this challenging question in different ways. Our Planet Tonight, and Thinglink, helped people to connect the small actions they might take as individuals to the bigger picture of why and how climate change is happening.

Two other Dott 07 projects, Landscape/Portrait and Town Crying, gave a face and voice to citizens who would otherwise be invisible statistics in planning and designing.

# Our Planet Tonight: how do we measure 'sustainable'? How far is it from here, to there?

Our Planet Tonight is an information design project to create a weather forecast equivalent for climate change. It was developed for the Dott 07 Festival in the style of a Radio One Roadshow. Professional and amateur TV presenters would take turns telling the story in three-minute segments, supported by an ecological and well-being 'dashboard'.

## Are we measuring what matters?

The biggest problem we confronted in Vital Signs was the sheer number of overlapping and sometimes contradictory indicators to choose from. Hundreds of organisations churn out a flood of reports, graphs, studies and punditry.

Some organisations focus on air quality and surface water quality. Others consider travel, energy use or how much we waste. And, for some scientists, potato yields or the egg-laying dates of birds are highly significant.

## A selection of indicators used to assess climate change across the UK[1]

- Air temperature in central England
- Seasonality of precipitation
- Precipitation gradient across the UK
- Predominance of westerly weather
- Dry and wet soil conditions in southern England
- Frequency of low and high river flows in North West and South East Britain
- Groundwater storage in the chalk in South East Britain
- Sea level rise
- The risk of tidal flooding in London
- Domestic property insurance claims for damaging weather events
- Supply of gas to households
- Scottish skiing industry
- Number of outdoor fires
- Incidence of Lyme disease in humans
- Seasonal pattern of human mortality
- Date of leaf emergence of trees in spring
- Health of beech trees in Britain
- Date of insect appearance and activity
- Arrival date of the swallow
- Egg-laying dates of birds
- Small bird population changes
- Marine plankton
- Upstream migration of salmon
- Appearance of ice on Lake Windermere

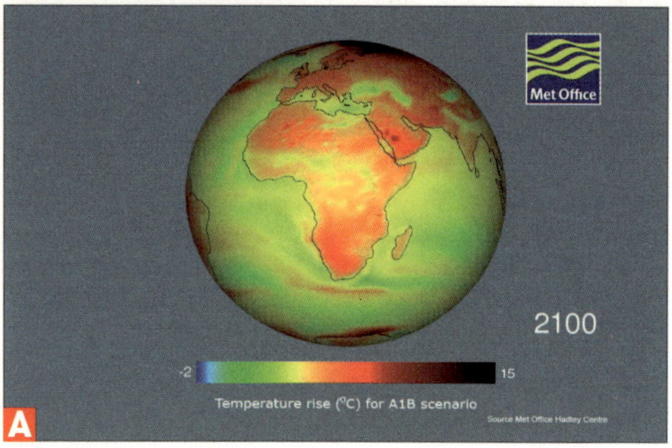


**A:** the Earth's surface temperature in the year 2100, as predicted in this powerful visualisation from the Hadley Centre

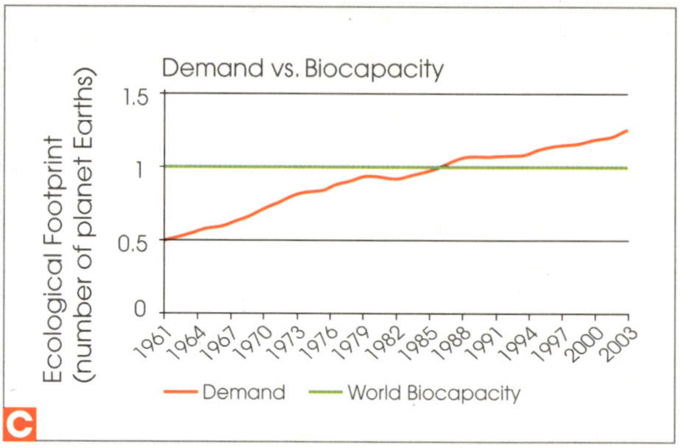


**C:** the capacity of the Earth's natural systems to absorb greenhouse gases – its 'carrying capacity' – is fixed. Man-made emissions, on the other hand, rise with our demand for goods and services

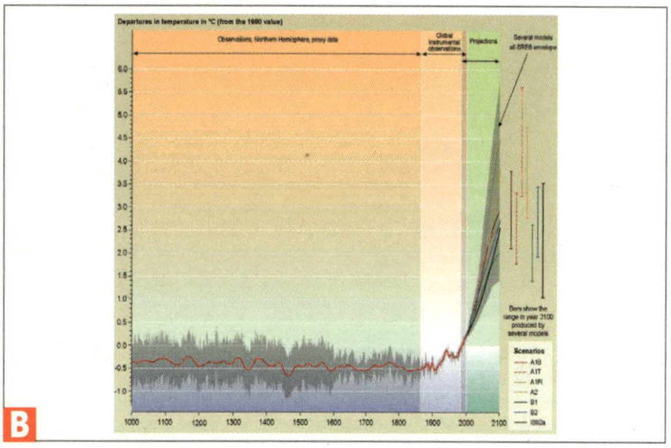


**B:** levels of $CO_2$ on Earth remained steady for 400,000 years – until the industrial age and carbon-based capitalism took off

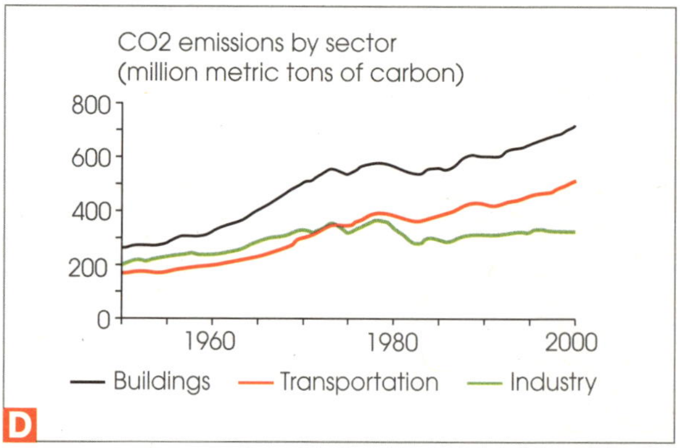


**D:** although industry gets a lot of the blame for greenhouse gas emissions, transportation – and especially buildings – do even more damage

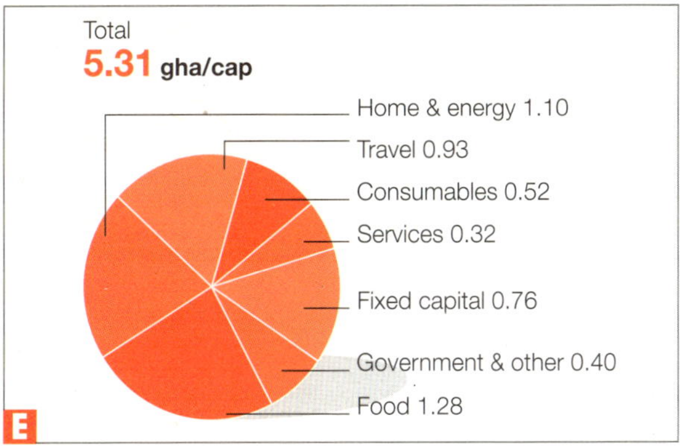


E: North East England's ecological footprint, as measured by the WWF

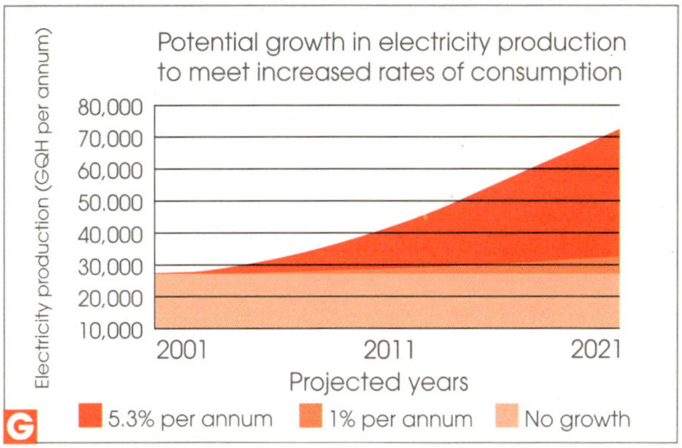


G: in common with other regions, the North East faces a sustainability dilemma: if its economy grows, so too does demand for electricity – and that means more $CO_2$ emissions

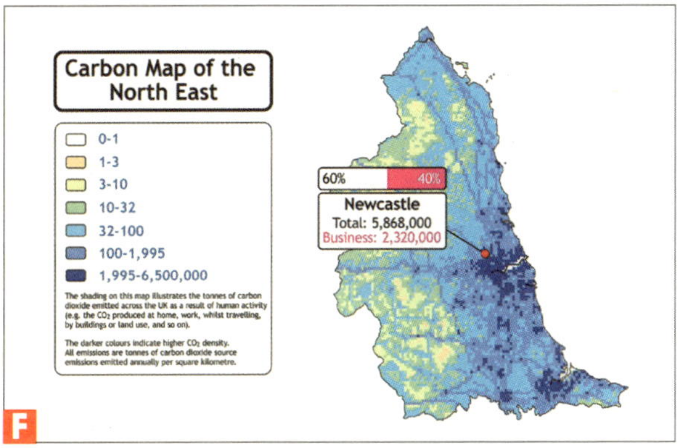


F: the Carbon Trust measured the North East's emissions by area. As the map shows, city regions like NewcastleGateshead make the biggest contribution to harmful emissions. Of course as big cities clean up their act, the savings can be bigger, too

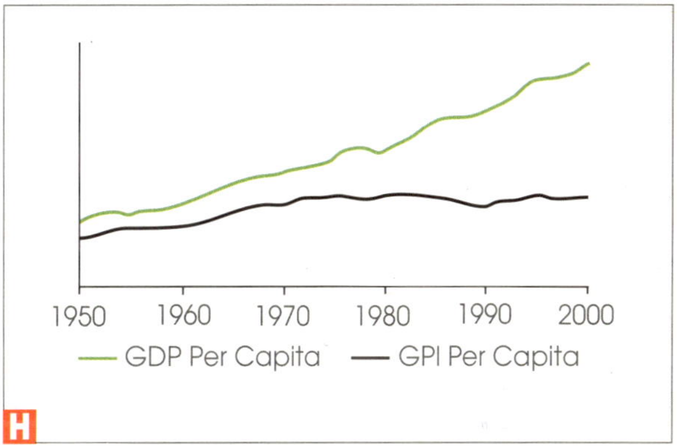


H: are we measuring what matters? Traditional measures of economic success focus on the GDP – the production of goods and services. New measures, such as the Happy Planet Index, show that people can live long, happy lives without using more than their fair share of the Earth's resources (www.happyplanetindex.org)

## What next?

Below is a list of useful websites related to this project:

Best Foot Forward www.bestfootforward.com
Carbon Trust www.carbontrust.co.uk
Met Office, Climate Change www.metoffice.gov.uk/research/hadleycentre/index.html
One Planet Living www.oneplanetliving.org
Happy Planet Index www.happyplanetindex.org
SEI – York: Regional Sustainability www.regionalsustainability.org

GRAPHICS: E & G – North East Counting Consumption by Alistair Paul, Aron Welch, John Barrett and Joe Ravetz. Partnered by WWF, Sei Cure and Biffaward. Published by WWF 2006; F – Carbon Trust; H – www.redefiningprogress.org

# Thinglink: what are the true environmental costs of that product – or banana?

Every product that enters our lives has a hidden history – an invisible 'rucksack' containing huge quantities of wasted or lost materials used in its production, transport, use and disposal.

## Every thing has a story

A great deal of nature has to be moved during the production of a computer. Many of its components require the use of high-grade minerals that can be obtained only through major mining operations and energy-intensive transformation processes. As Amory Lovins, Paul Hawken and Hunter Lovins – the authors of *Natural Capitalism* – explain, industry uses billions of pounds of material in order to manufacture the products we take for granted, and to construct the roads and buildings and infrastructures needed to deliver them.

Added up over a year, the amount of matter and energy wasted, or caused to be wasted, by the average North American consumer is roughly a million pounds in weight[2]. Europeans are better, but not by much.

These are not rumours. The material flows of our industrial society, its 'metabolism', have been measured with growing accuracy in recent times.

'Every thing has a story. We help people to link to it,' says Finnish designer and system developer Ulla-Maaria Mutanen. Mutanen created Thinglink to be an open online database for anyone, from artists to designers, collectors and trendspotters, to add and publish portfolios with their favourite things.

For a presentation at the Dott Festival, Mutanen's Thinglink team explored how their basic concept could be combined with mobile phones so that you or I would be able to scan products and read their environmental credentials before purchase.

**The amount of waste matter generated in the manufacture of a single laptop computer is close to 4,000 times its weight on your lap[3]**

**Thinglink provides a way to 'read' the size of a product's ecological rucksack by scanning it with a mobile phone**

## Where do the numbers come from?

Some companies and government departments are guilty of 'greenwashing'. Greenwashing occurs when companies (or governments) spend more money or time on advertising their green credentials than on investing in environmentally sound practices.

This is where the Publicly Available Specification, or PAS, comes in. Think of a PAS as a product's ecological passport. The Carbon Trust and the UK's Environment Ministry, Defra, have joined with the British Standards Institution (BSI) to develop a standard method for measuring the embodied greenhouse gas emissions in all products and services.

If every product or service were required to display a PAS that we could read with our mobile phones, it would enable people to make a meaningful comparison between the environmental performance of competing products and services.

New rules to regulate 'offsetting' are also in the pipeline. The UK government has plans to launch a new offsetting code.

Carbon offsetting is the act of mitigating ('offsetting') greenhouse gas emissions. A well-known example is the planting of trees to compensate for the greenhouse gas emissions from personal air travel. Other offset methods are now in use: renewable energy and energy conservation offsets have gained popularity.

As governments and international institutions respond to political pressure and impose order on environmental reporting systems, designers such as Ulla-Maaria Mutanen can make data widely accessible in creative ways.

*Greenwashing is when a company (or government) spends more money or time on advertising its green credentials than on investing in environmentally sound practices*

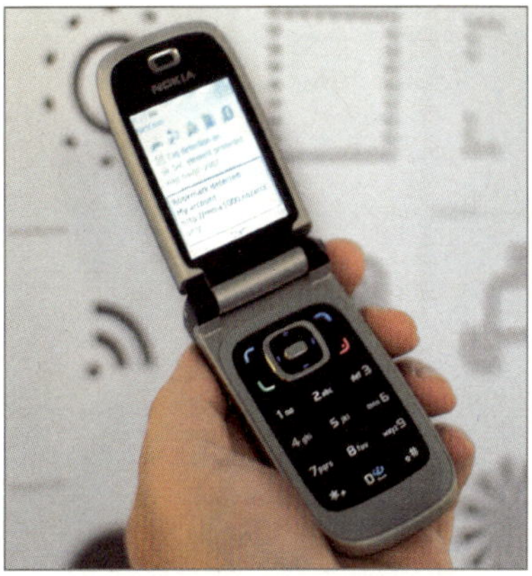

**Above:** Thinglink proposes a way of downloading the ecological data relating to any product using your mobile phone

### What next?

To keep track of developments in the design of ways to read the history of products on our mobile phones, check these websites:

**Thinglink** http://thinglink.org

**Publicly Available Specification (PAS)** www.defra.gov.uk/news/2007/070530a.htm

**Near Field Communication (NFC)** http://en.wikipedia.org/wiki/Near_Field_Communication

**Tool for Sustainable Consumption (MIPS)** www.cleanproduction.org/Steps.Products.Life.MIPS.php

# Town Crying: how can we be heard?

**Wouldn't it be great if...** a series of public performances started conversations about people's design aspirations for the places in which they live?

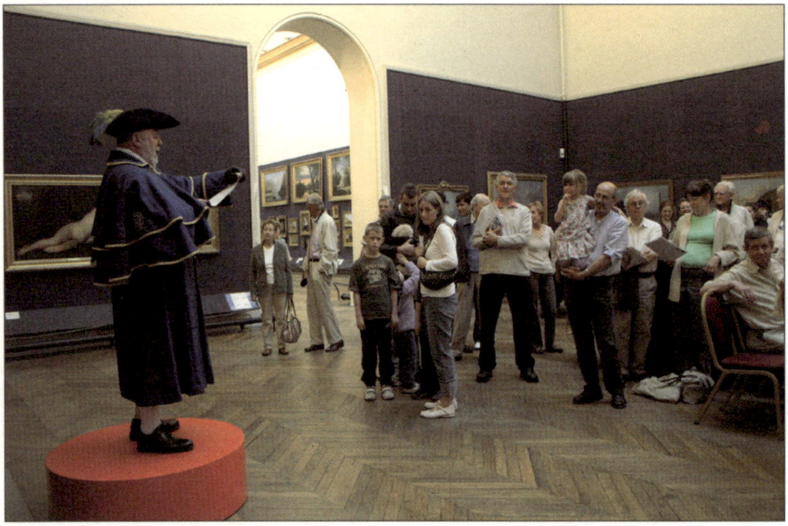

## About town criers

The Town Crying project drew on the tradition of town criers announcing local news, events and other matters of commercial and legal interest. The practice became popular in medieval England and was used here until the late 18th century. Its original form can be traced back to ancient Greece.

Today, town crying is used mainly as a heritage event though criers are often hired for private functions. To this day it is a criminal offence to interrupt, heckle or otherwise trouble a working town crier.

## How did Dott's Town Crying project work?

Working with Alnwick's award-winning town crier John Stevens, performance art group Lone Twin were commissioned by Forma to create a series of proclamations to be 'cried' across North East England. The texts told stories of places, events and communities, compiled during a period of research in the area, which included discussions with local inhabitants, workers and passers-by.

Each proclamation gave a sense of the eclectic nature of local life by combining hearsay, first-person accounts, factual narrative and fictional construct. The audiences were a combination of people who followed the performances to each new destination and those who came across them by chance.

This project formed part of North East England's world-class festival and events programme.

**Left:** the Alnwick town crier in action
**Opposite:** the proclamations told stories of places, events and communities compiled during a period of research in the area

## What next?

A book containing reproductions of the scripts and full-colour photos of performances was distributed free to all visitors to the Dott 07 Festival.

Below is a list of useful websites related to this project:

**Lone Twin** www.lonetwin.com
**Alnwick Town Crier** www.alnwicktowncrier.com
**Forma** www.forma.org.uk
**Town Crying** www.dott07.com/go/vitalsigns

PHOTO: Ginny Reed

# IN THE ACT OF KILLING A DRAGON WITH HIS LANCE

**Oyez, Oyez, Oyez. This area is not a toilet. Oyez, Oyez, Oyez.**

Inside the very building looming behind me, a woman, lost in the endless aisles of John Lewis, is approached by a shop assistant:
- Are you looking for something?
- Yes, I am looking for my husband.

It is the end of the world! Is this how we live? We look for our husbands in John Lewis? Ladies and Gentlemen of Old Eldon Square, boys and girls of the EMO, sons and daughters of the Goth, hidden souls of the Hoody and the wingless creatures of the Bus Shelter, is this it? Is this how we live?
We meet in a square, in a city, in the great North East and we stand together.

**Oyez, Oyez, Oyez. We wait, we watch, we text Sandra. Oyez, Oyez, Oyez.**

Wingless creatures of the Bus Shelter gone are the days of the George and Dragon.
Gone are the days of the half and the pie.
These are the days of the Wagamama.
Regard the figure of St. George and his slain dragon regarding the days of the Wagamama.
Regard his British Lion, his justice, his peace, his chicken chilli noodles.
Who here fights for peace? Who here once worked for River Island, but now, with child, moves to Australia? Who here said "I can't stay here, it's too much, too many fights, it's just too much"?
Who here longs to leave, who here longs for the number 39 to Dumpling Hall?

**Oyez, Oyez, Oyez. Stand with us. Oyez, Oyez, Oyez.**

To the boys and girls of the EMO, sons and daughters of the Goth, hidden souls of the Hoody, the wingless creatures of the Bus Shelter, and the society of the society of the Café Society. You meet in a square, in a city, in the great North East, you take a frappuccino, you take chicken chilli noodles, you take a breath and you say: I used to come here and stand with the kids, I was on my own, I wore a Guns N' Roses tee shirt and some Goths looked at me and said, 'Alright mate you can stand with us'.
Ladies and Gentlemen this is how we live. Stand with us.

God save She Who Lost Her Husband, God save She Who Moves To Australia, God save He for Whom The Fighting Is Too Much, God save He Who Listens To Guns N' Roses, God save The Queen!

TOWN CRYING
A LONE TWIN PROJECT

19.07.07 OLD ELDON SQUARE

# Landscape/Portrait: do the statistics used by planners represent real people?

**Wouldn't it be great if...** the faces and voices of citizens influenced design and regeneration projects – not just abstract data?

Does your postcode define who you are? Statistical models of communities based on postcode areas are often used in the design and planning of public services and regeneration projects.

Landscape/Portrait confronts people living in the North East with their demographic 'stereotype' based on these statistics and asks them 'Is this you?'.

## How did it work?

In Landscape/Portrait, Forma commissioned media artist Kevin Carter, working with Media 19, to present three communities across the region with demographic stereotypes about their own area.

People from within these communities then worked with Kevin and Media 19 to create a series of video self-portraits. These were presented as part of a outdoor campaign and uploaded to a purpose-built website, alongside the official statistical data and stereotypes currently held by market research agencies about each location.

The campaign aimed to entice people to contribute to the online community, where they could create and upload their own video portraits. This online community was then exhibited at the Dott 07 festival, where visitors could use a laptop and webcam to create their own portraits live on site.

The website presents participants with a fictional character who asks a series of questions about where they live, who they are, their health, hobbies, happiness, work and aspirations for themselves and their neighbourhood. The interview is recorded live via a webcam, then automatically uploaded to the website.

The site maps each portrait geographically and allows visitors to search for portraits by postcode, username or questions answered. Visitors to the site are encouraged to leave comments under the profiles to open up discussion and debate.

Landscape/Portrait invites citizens to think about who they are, how they are and how they would like their communities to be.

This project formed part of North East England's world-class festival and events programme.

## What next?

Landscape/Portrait was produced for Dott 07 by Forma as a collaboration between artist Kevin Carter, Media 19, and the University of Teesside.

Dott 07 festival visitors were invited to view and respond to their own personal video portraits. In this process, which is ongoing, the project evaluates demographic data by comparing them to the lives of citizens and communities across the region.

To generate your own profile and join the debate from home, you will need a broadband internet connection and a webcam.

Below is a list of useful websites related to this project:

**Landscape/Portrait**
www.landscape-portrait.com
www.dott07.com/go/landscape
**Co Lab Projects**
www.co-lab.org/commissions
**Forma** www.forma.org.uk
**Media 19** www.media19.co.uk

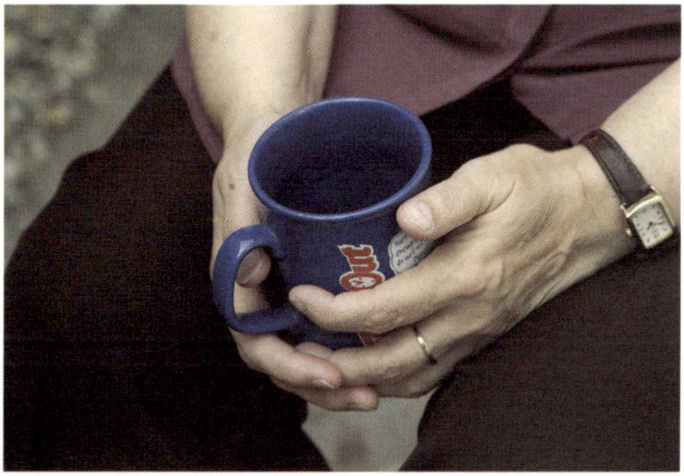

YOU ARE EITHER OVER 60 OR UNDER 16, YOU ARE UNEMPLOYED, YOU DON'T EARN MUCH, YOU GO TO BINGO OR HAVE A BET AT THE BOOKIES.

DOES YOUR POSTCODE DEFINE WHO YOU ARE?

Visit www.landscape-portrait.com to find out.

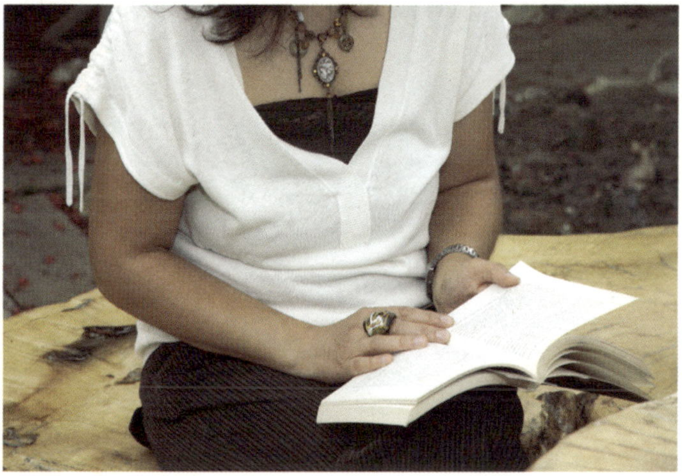

YOU ARE AFFLUENT, YOUR HOUSE IS LARGE, YOU HAVE TWO CARS, YOU ENJOY WALKING, PLAYING GOLF AND GOING TO THE GYM YOU HAVE SHARES.

DOES YOUR POSTCODE DEFINE WHO YOU ARE?

Visit www.landscape-portrait.com to find out.

**Above:** Landscape/Portrait presented people with a series of demographic 'stereotypes', and asked them 'Is this you?'

PHOTOS: Karin Coetzee

# Movement: can transport and tourism be sustainable?

The movement of people and goods around the world consumes vast amounts of matter, energy, space and time. Could transport intensity be separated from economic progress – and, if so, how?

**People are badly informed about existing public transport services: we overestimate by 70% the potential length of a journey by public transport – and underestimate the length of a car journey by 26%[4]**

**What price transportation?**

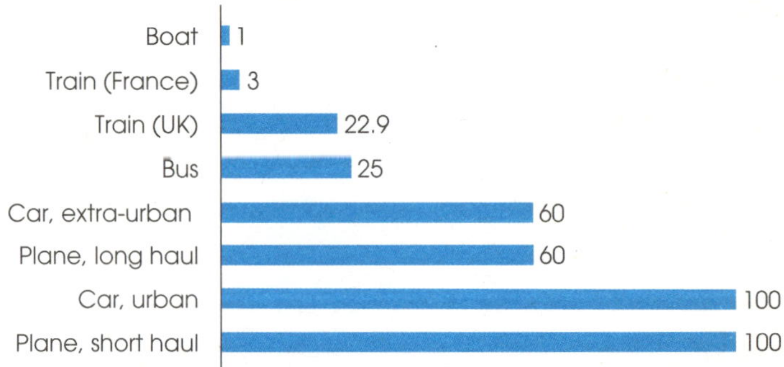


Greenhouse gas emisssions per passenger per km, for different means of transportation (in grams carbon equivalent).

BAR CHART: ADEME & INRETS / manicore.com

# Move Me: could we get where we need to go without new cars and roads?

**Wouldn't it be great if...** we could go where we need to go using transport options that already exist but are under-used? No car? No problem!

## How we move in Scremerston

The Move Me project centred on Scremerston First School in Northumberland. Three miles from Berwick, this small school is a daily hub for 42 children and 34 families. It also has 11 members of staff, including full- and part-time teachers, cleaning, catering and janitorial staff, and is led by an enthusiastic head teacher, Helen Harrison, who was keen for the school to be fully involved in the project.

The school's many and varied transport needs made it an excellent test case for Dott 07. The project looked at the school community's mobility needs and explored how they could be better served by combining existing services in smarter ways – for example, the planning of integrated journeys, vehicle sharing, or better use of community vehicles such as minibuses. Ultimately, the project team aimed to design a reliable and sustainable transport service that would help this particular rural community and also provide a model that would work elsewhere.

The project was linked to a wider initiative called RAMP (Rural Access and Mobility Project), which looked at a similar set of issues in the field of healthcare access. Move Me was an excellent opportunity to apply some of the findings from RAMP to a new group of users.

**Transport accounts for 20% of the average school's carbon footprint[5]**

**Newcastle was rated the noisiest urban area in England, with traffic noise measured at 80.4 decibels[6]. That's like a loud alarm clock constantly ringing in a person's ear**

*'I'd like to go to an after-school club, but it's too far away for Dad to pick me up afterwards'*

## How does Move Me work?

The Move Me project team began by gathering insights from the Scremerston community. David Townson and Richard Telford from live | work, the design and innovation company producing Move Me, developed travel activity packs for the pupils of Scremerston First School to help build a picture of how and why they travelled the way they did.

The packs included seven short tasks, including 'Me and my family – tell us about you and who you live with', 'I like to go... – tell us about places you enjoy going to outside of school time' and 'Interview a parent – ask a parent questions all about travel'. Pupils took the packs home and filled them in with the help of their parents.

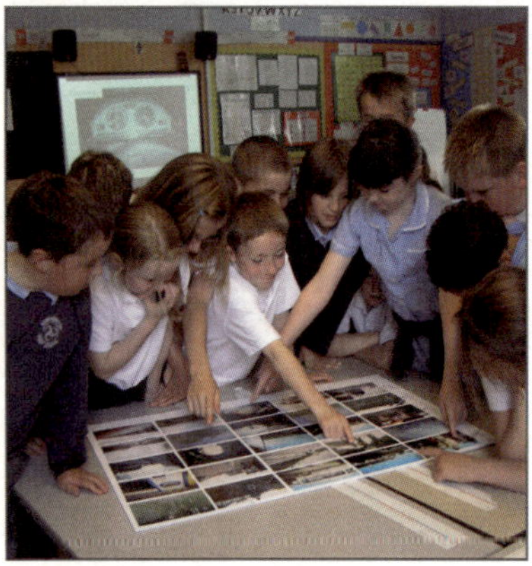

Above: pupils at Scremerston school provided insights into local transport options

Feedback from the activity packs included the following revelations:

- Most pupils are driven to school either because the bus doesn't go to their area or they live too far away.
- 72% of parents thought the school should encourage less use of cars for school journeys.
- 57% of parents never take the children of other families to school.
- 69% of parents who never take children from other families to school would consider it.

Major problem areas included: infrequency of buses; the limited service of the current school bus run; the expense of taxis; unfair fares; and confusing public transport timetables. The questions also unearthed a variety of individual problems with getting to and from schools, after-school clubs, Sure Start classes, dental appointments and the town facilities at Berwick, such as clinics and shops.

Having gathered the information, the live | work team started to develop solutions that would not involve putting any new vehicles on the road. In April, they met with the community to discuss their ideas and highlight their own solutions.

Two early solutions were developed from the initial research:

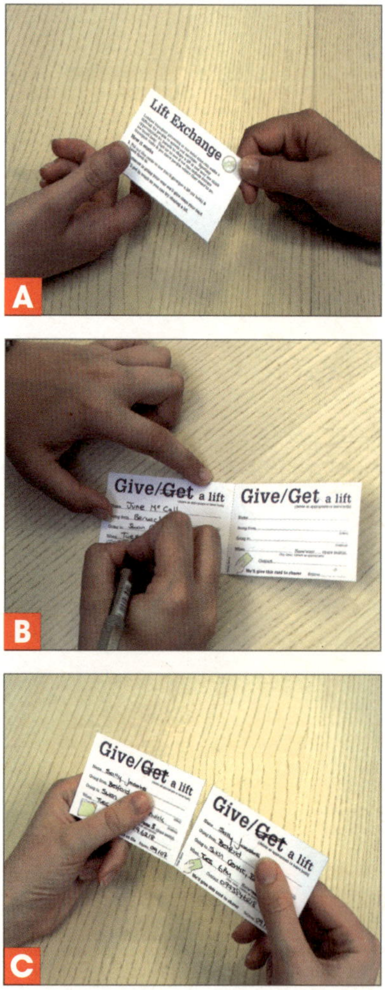


**Above:** during Move Me, live | work developed and trialled a series of low-cost, paper-based templates including 'lift exchange' cards (see above) for community service providers – from midwives to football coaches – to improve access to their services

ILLUSTRATION: live | work

• Improve existing bus services. Arriva, a local bus provider, worked with live | work and the community to improve its service by introducing a new user-friendly, colour-coded bus timetable.

• Create a toolkit for service providers: the kit consists of a number of simple paper-based tools that aim to help providers increase the number of people accessing their service by making it easier to get there.

Providers are able to set up a lift-sharing scheme that encourages people to offer and request lifts to their venue. It is hoped that this 'offline' scheme will complement the Northumberland Car Share site (www.northumberlandcarshare.com) and ultimately lead to increased use of this currently under-used community resource.

The Move Me team took its lift-share toolkit to community class leaders over the summer and it is currently being trialled with over 2000 people through working with Scremerston First School, Sure Start Berwick Borough (who provide support to parents and children) and Berwick Community Centre (who run adult education classes).

The team also visited Scremerston First School over the summer to work with children on completing the design activity they had started in January when they filled in their travel packs. The results were shared with the children, who were encouraged to design posters illustrating the advantages of sharing lifts, riding their bikes to school and taking the bus.

**Below:** live | work developed this interactive transport map for the Dott 07 Festival. It is designed to illustrate the potential environmental and financial savings that people could achieve by sharing lifts with other people

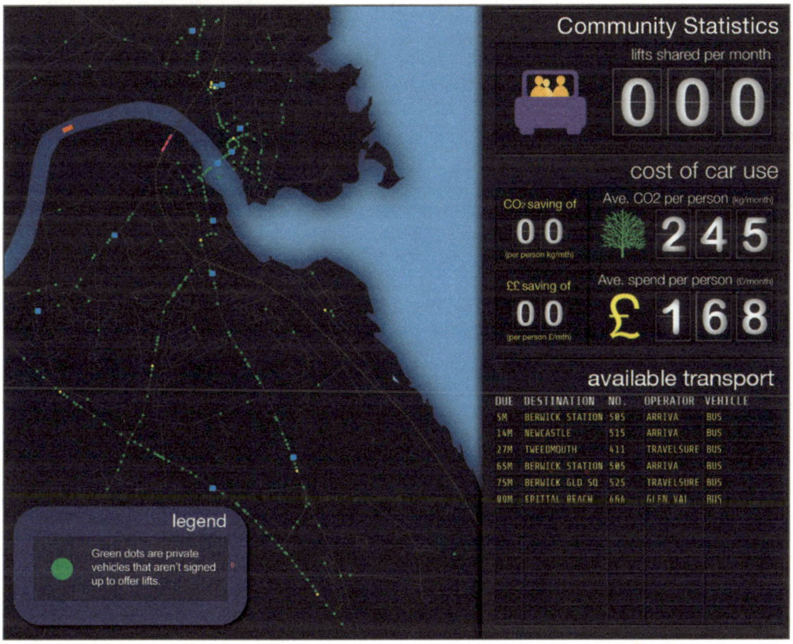


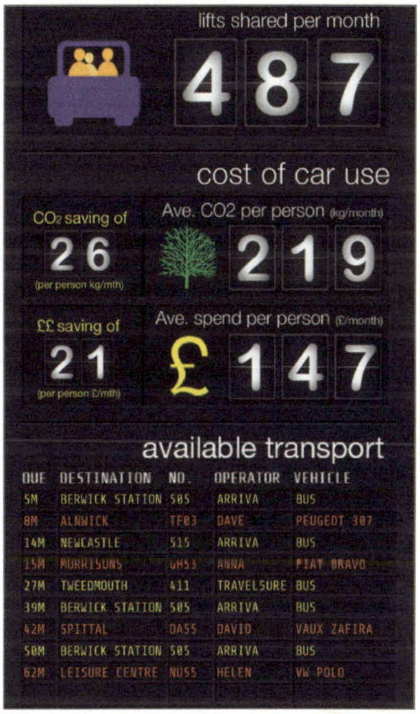

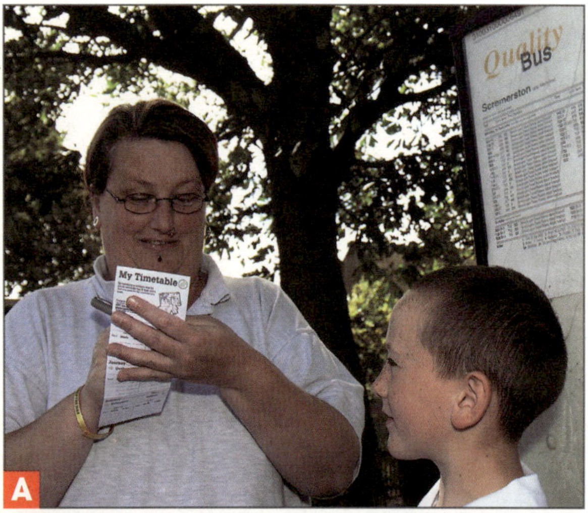


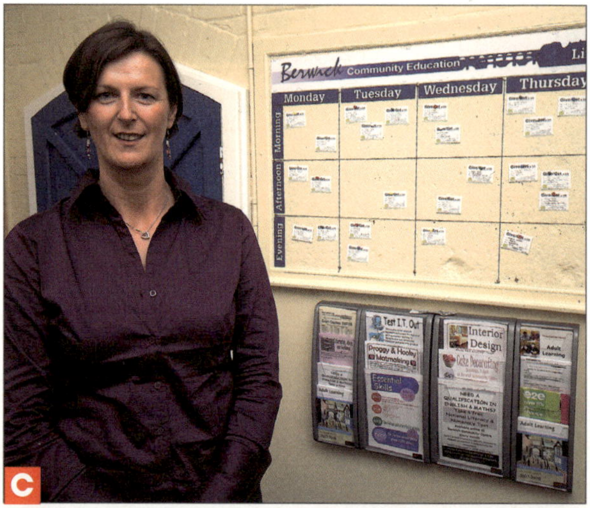


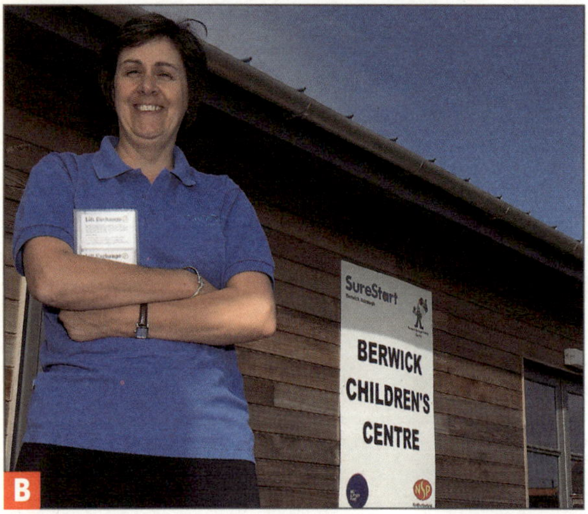


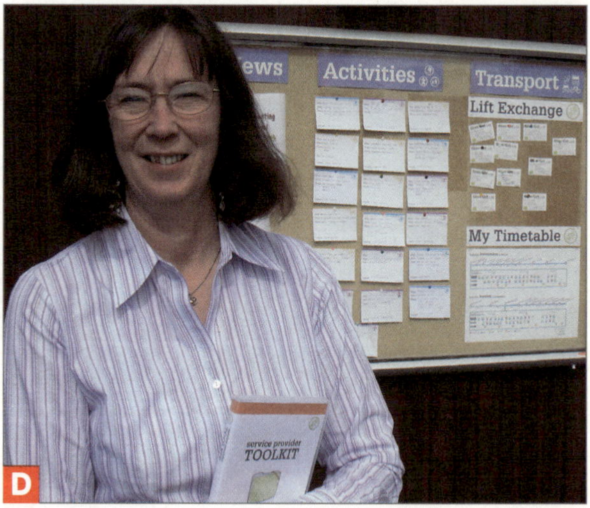


A: Margaret and Peter, Scremerston First School – Margaret and her son Peter are using My Timetable: handy cards to record the times for transport that they need for the journeys they make

B. Carolynn Reavley, Sure Start midwife – Sure Start are also trialling Lift Exchange, in which midwives collect travel information and match parents offering and requesting lifts to its venues

C. Fiona Hall, Berwick Community Centre – Berwick Community Centre is trialling Lift Exchange, a way for its 1,800 students to post offers and requests for transport to and from classes

D. Helen Harrison, Scremerston First School – Scremerston First School are using every element of the Service Provider Toolkit to provide parents with information about local services and the support to access them

PHOTOS: live|work

## Helen Harrison

**Head teacher, Scremerston First School in Northumberland**

**What would a better transport system mean for the school?**
'Small schools in Northumberland are a hub for the villages, not just for the children but for everyone who lives here. Improved access and easier transport could ultimately increase numbers at the school and increase the viability of our small, but highly rated, school. We have lost children due to the poor transport links.

'Currently, we have one particularly gifted child who lives outside the catchment area. The family doesn't have a car and aren't very well off, so they need to take a taxi to get to the school. They don't want to move school, but may have to because of the expense. And we didn't see one boy in pre-school for two weeks because his father's car broke down and he couldn't get him here any other way.'

**What changes would you like to see?**
'I would want to see the children have broader and richer cultural experiences through being able to access places such as the theatre, sports centre, drama groups and places of interest such as Holy Island.

'Generally, I would like to see them getting more education outside of the school. Being from a village and growing up here shouldn't mean that you can't experience other things.'

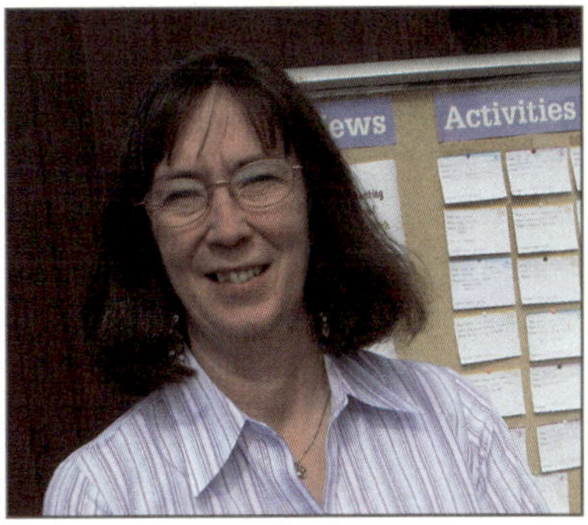


**What difference would it make to the life of the village?**
'Better transport to the village would probably increase the number of people living here. People are understandably put off because there's no shop or pub.

'More people would mean more children at the school, but would also mean a more vibrant life here for everybody.'

### What next?

'Move Me' project outcomes include a toolkit for transport providers who wish to improve access to their services. The toolkit includes 'Lift Exchange' cards, 'Activity Templates' for notice boards, and personalised 'My Timetable' forms.

The lessons of Move Me, whch was led by live | work, will also feed into the Rural Access and Mobility Project (RAMP) which fosters sustainable approaches to rural transport in the North East.

For more information, go to www.dott07.com/go/moveme or email Laura Lomax on laura@livework.co.uk

Other useful websites include:
**live | work** www.livework.co.uk
**NorthumberlandCar Share** www.northumberlandcarshare.com
**Sustrans, UK sustainable transport charity** www.sustrans.org.uk
**Lift Share**
Car sharing schemes for communities www.liftshare.org
**Car share services**
www.streetcar.co.uk
www.whizzgo.co.uk
**Go Loco**
Service on Facebook that helps people share rides between friends, neighbours, and colleagues and share trip costs online)
www.goloco.org/index
**New Mobility 177 Ideas for Sustainable Transportation**
www.ecoplan.org/wtpp/wt_index.htm
**Sustainable Transportation**
http://en.wikipedia.org/wiki/sustainable_transportation
**Time Pollution essay by John Whitelegg** www.worldcarfree.net/resources/freesources/polluti.htm

# Sustainable tourism: must tourism damage the toured?

**Wouldn't it be great if...** we had more examples of sustainable tourism on which to build?

**In carbon footprint terms, one holiday in New Zealand is equivalent to 60 short visits to the North East[7]. But 60 more holidays in Newcastle will not be sustainable if they require investment in heavy new infrastructure and/or promote wasteful behaviour by the visitor**

## Radical ideas, real locations

This international design camp, led by Steve Messam, brought together teams of young designers, senior students, visual artists, architects and young professionals to develop sustainable tourism ideas for (and with) specific North East locations and communities.

Participants came from eight different countries and spanned many disciplines. Their projects looked at everything from urban camping to the structures that are likely to emerge with the advent of geothermal energy, and the decoration of landscape using the tools and patterns of agriculture.

The teams were allocated to four locations across the North East of England and asked to investigate how sustainable tourism might be developed and implemented there. They worked with local partners to document the features of value in the area.

Tasks included:

- Describing how visitors might experience this feature in new ways
- Creating an opportunity map of places, or services, to be designed
- Creating artefacts and/or a storyboard of a proposed new service or situation
- Describing the business or enterprise model that would make their proposal truly sustainable.

Throughout the 10-day camp, the teams worked with co-ordinators and the local community to tackle the design challenges. Various experts from around the world acted as mentors to the teams through a series of day and evening sessions.

**Your holiday travel footprint**

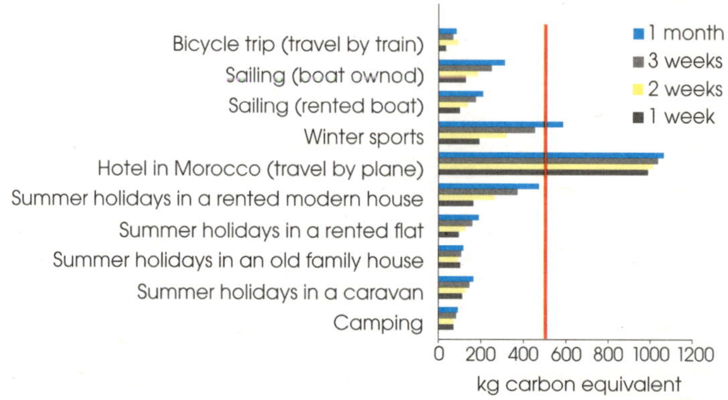


BAR CHART: Manicore ILLUSTRATION: Design Camp – Urban Camping team

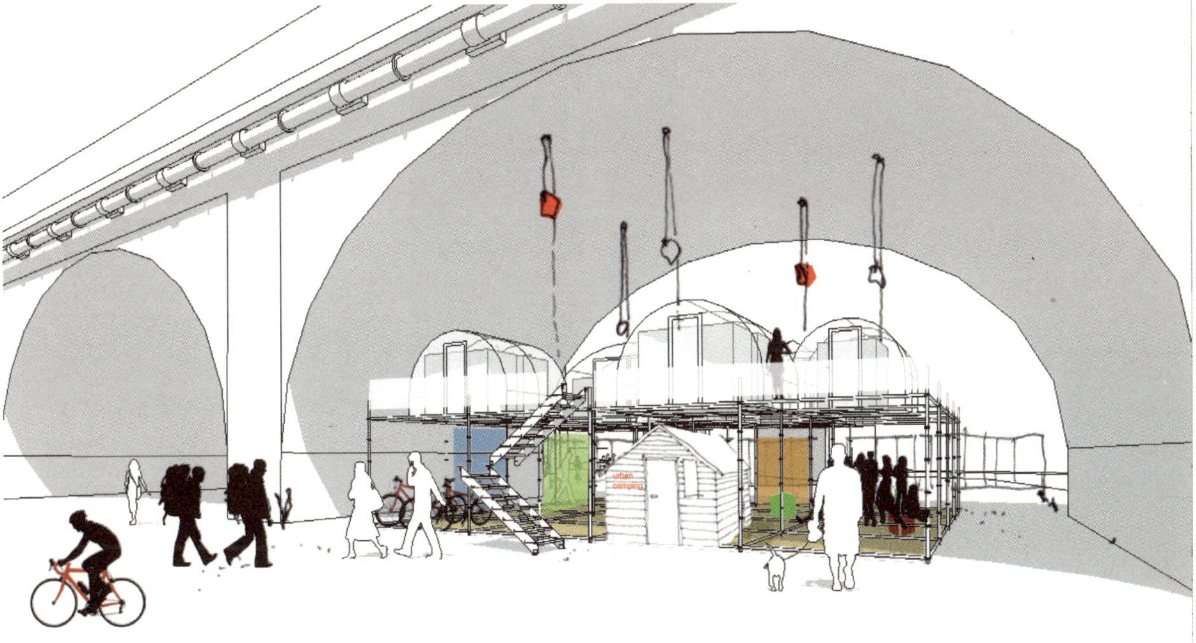


## Urban camping

Exploring the concept of urban camping and 'camp&ride' schemes as a model for sustainable urban tourism, the first group worked on an urban camping brief. Their aim was to transform a disused space in NewcastleGateshead into sustainable accommodation for visitors to the Dott 07 Festival in October. The team envisaged a huge tent space based in an archway beneath Byker Bridge, which would protect the visitor from the North's October weather. Tents would sit on platforms of varied heights within the cocoon.

The area would be electricity-free and would have a communal cooking and eating area to encourage sharing and conversation, as well as a more relaxed beanbag seating area.

The group looked beyond the physical to design with the entire experience in mind: a local man and his dog – 'Bob and the Dog' – were to welcome people to the campsite and act as security, Quaylink buses were to bring people from Central Station to Ouseburn and the local business RecykeY' Bike was to provide recycled red Dott 07 bikes for visitors to explore the city.

**Above:** how a disused city space might be transformed into a contemporary, ecologically-friendly campsite

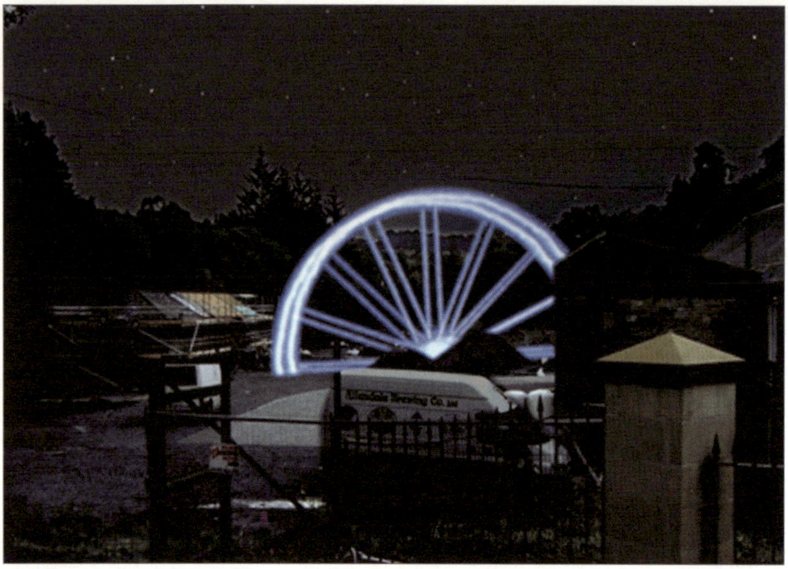

**Left:** the Allendale Industrial Heritage team proposed recreating a spectacular water wheel on an old smelt mill as a night-time light installation

## Allendale Industrial Heritage

The second design camp group worked with the rural community and industrial heritage of the North Pennines on a project entitled 'Revealing the Invisible'. The concept involved staging night-time outdoor light installations, highlighting industrial structures that have become ruined or have disappeared completely. The centrepieces of the light installations were all features of Allendale's lead mining heritage and community, including a long-demolished aqueduct, a spectacular water wheel on the old smelt mill, and the Blackett level, a long, straight, underground tunnel.

Audiences were particularly taken with the team's interpretation of two largely ruined round stone chimneys, which were 'virtually' recreated using strong beams of bright, blue light shone from inside the structures to represent their original height.

## Landlines – Designing the agricultural landscape

How could minor changes to farming procedures change the face of the landscape? This was the question the Landlines team asked themselves while working with farmers to explore how existing resources might be used to change the view from the windows of Mainline trains travelling through the North East. The aim of the project was also to underline the roles of farmers as producers and custodians of the landscape.

The Landlines project will be ongoing over the next 18 months (see what next?, *right*).

**Below:** a montage of rapeseed in Northumberland (where the Landlines project was based) and wild flowers in the Indres, France

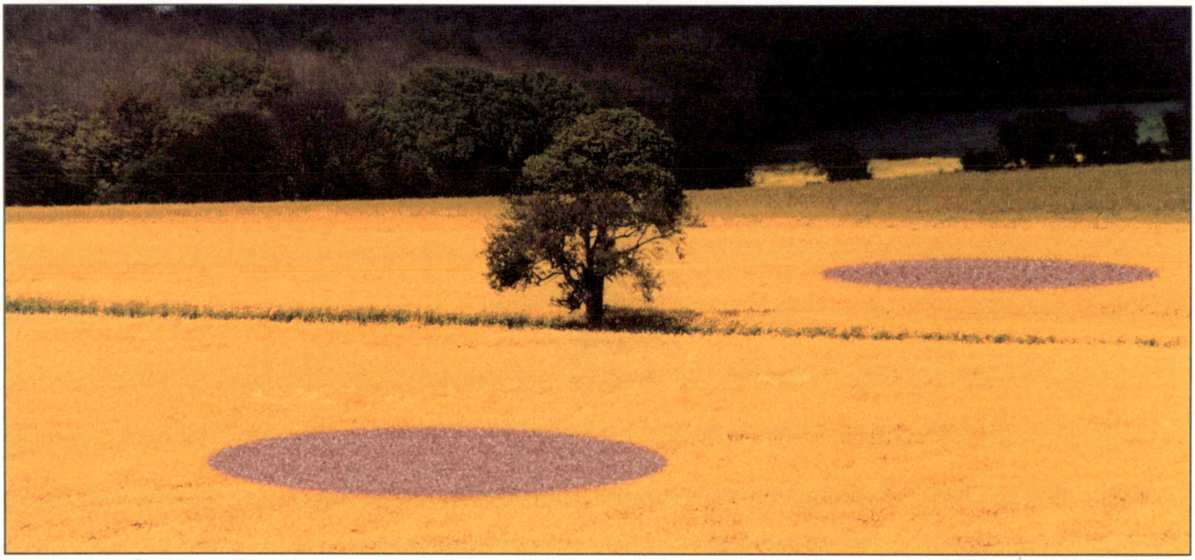

PHOTOS: Night wheel – Allendale team; Landlines – Steve Messam

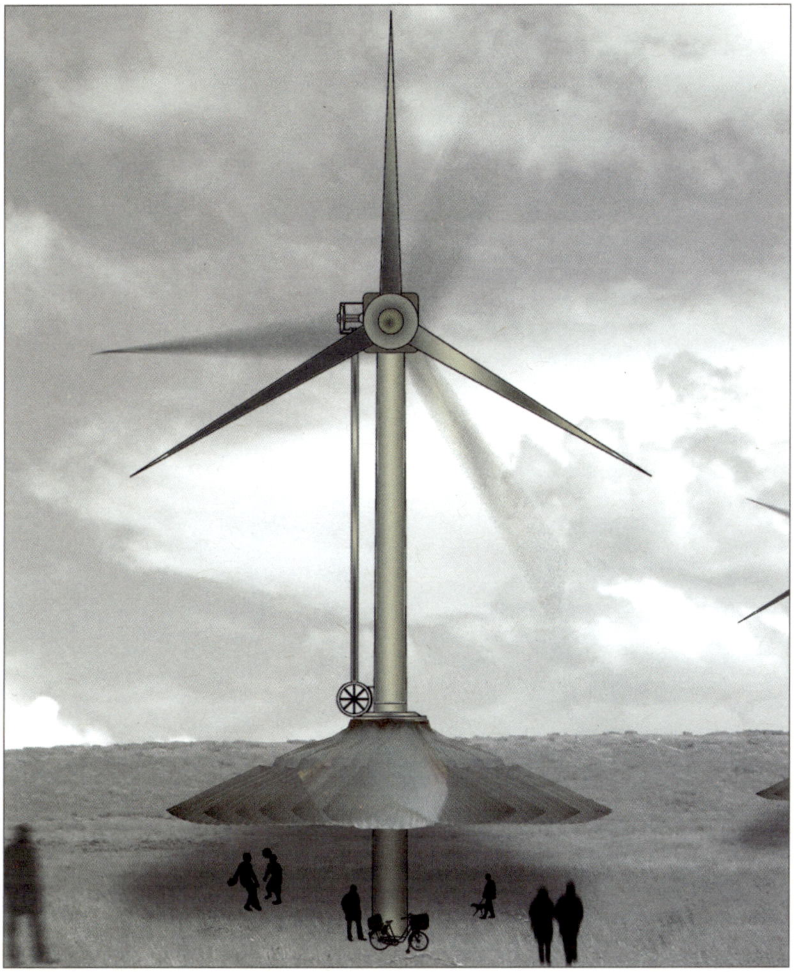

## What next?

Everyone can become a more sustainable tourist. The key is to make use of local resources in ways that provide benefit to the community without damaging the local environment. In a sustainable region, we will make better use of the people and heritage that are already here.

Below is a list of useful websites related to this project:

**Landlines** www.foldgallery.co.uk

**Tyne Salmon Trail**
www.xsitearchitecture.co.uk

**Seat 61 – gets you anywhere in the world without flying**
www.seat61.com

For more information, go to www.dott07.com/go/designcamp

## Wind Power in the Landscape

The final project explored the concept of power generation as visual spectacle and tourist attraction. It asked: can wind power have a positive effect on the landscape and tourism? Are wind farms examples of contemporary beauty or monstrosities obstructing the view?

The group developed an unusual way of communicating the power of these huge structures, thereby creating a reason for tourists and local residents alike to visit the site. The rotation of each turbine would turn a huge 'skirt' of material suspended around its trunk. Visitors could gather beneath the whirling installation – named *Perpetua* – and use the space to meet others, hold events or watch the world go by.

**Above:** the wind power team envisaged a whirling installation designed to exploit the visual attributes of wind farms

ILLUSTRATION: Wind turbine – Team Wind

# Picture House: how can we make more of our cultural heritage?

**Wouldn't it be great if...** we were able to experience historic houses in fresh ways?

## Picture House

So you think you know what an English country house feels like? Well, think again. Film directors, artists and designers transformed Belsay Hall in Northumberland with a series of cutting-edge art and new media installations.

In a sustainable region, we can make better use of the people and heritage that are already there. Three Dott projects in Picture House provoked us to look at familiar situations in fresh ways.

English Heritage curator Judith King and Dott 07, together with Juha Huuskonen, invited experimental film directors, artists and designers to transform Belsay Hall in Northumberland through a series of art and new media work in Belsay's vast empty rooms, spare castle and Grade I-listed gardens.

## Who took part in Picture House for Dott?

**United Visual Artists (UVA): *Hereafter***
UVA is a company of artists, recorders and designers who usually work within the music industry and with bands such as Massive Attack. For Belsay, UVA created a 'history mirror'. The installation reflected both the images of visitors present and those who had previously visited. The result was a constantly changing and mysterious visual display.

**Adam Somlai-Fischer and Bengt Sjölén: *The Gardens***
Bengt Sjölén (Sweden) and Adam Somlai-Fischer (Hungary) created *The Gardens* at Picture House to draw attention to the spectacular array of colours in Belsay's formal gardens. The installation was made from 200

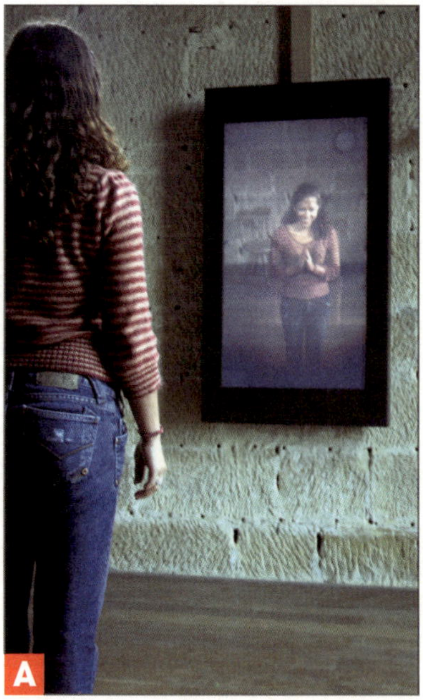

A: UVA's *Hereafter*

**Acknowledgement**
Picture House, Film, Art and Design at Belsay, was presented by English Heritage as part of its contemporary art programme in the North East, which is funded by Northern Rock Foundation and Arts Council England, North East. The Picture House exhibition was also funded by Design Council England, Esmee Fairbairn Foundation, Heritage Lottery Fund, Northumberland Strategic Partnership and One NorthEast, and formed part of the North East England World Class Festival and Events Programme and Dott 07.

PHOTOS: A, B & D – Andy Taylor

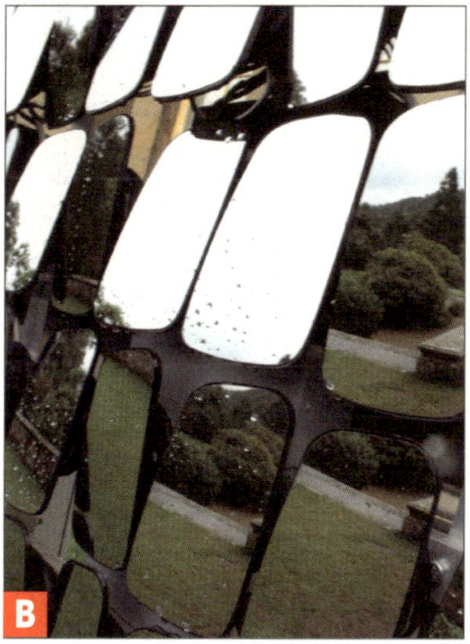

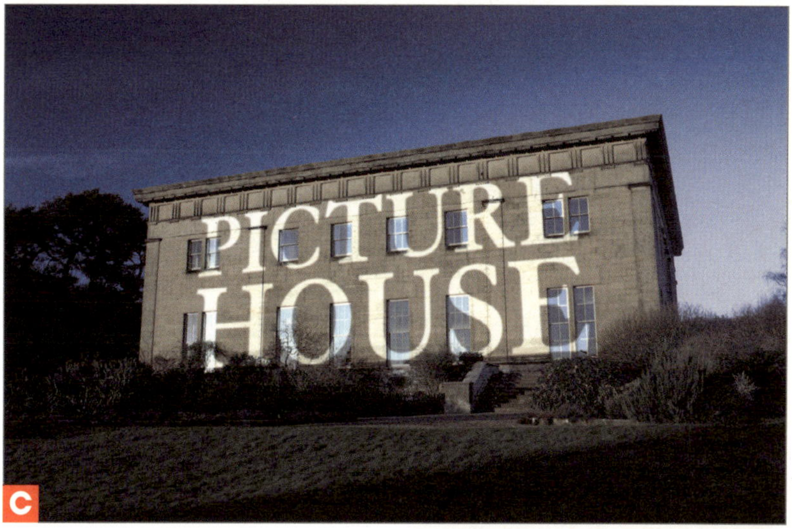


B: *The Gardens/Aleph* – a kinetic reflection display system
C: Belsay Hall, Northumberland
D: Levin's *Ghost Pole Propagator*

Citroën ZX electric mirrors controlled by cameras and computers. Each mirror reflected a fragment of the whole in a matrix of reds, greens and purples. The result blurred the distinctions between architecture, people and media.

Somlai-Fischer and Sjölén called the 'kinetic reflection display' system in their installation *Aleph*. The name *Aleph* refers to a fictional point of singularity created by Argentine author Jorge Luis Borges. The artists explained that a point in space contains all other points. The idea is that anyone who gazes into it can see everything in the universe from every angle simultaneously, without distortion, overlapping or confusion.

**Golan Levin:**
***Ghost Pole Propagator***

Celebrated new-media artist Golan Levin created *Ghost Pole Propagator*, an interactive software artwork that was installed in a deserted castle in Belsay Hall's grounds. The artwork captures and replays the 'skeletons' of passers-by in its environment.

The effect was a dynamic show in which animated, but abstract, figures replicated the gestures of visitors' movements and their gait, while re-processing the images in more abstract ways.

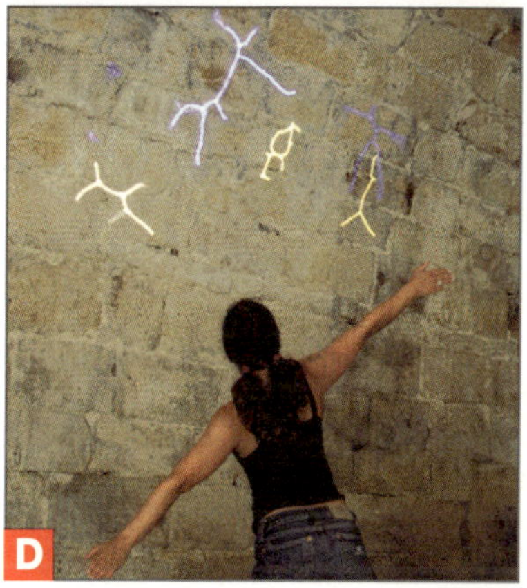

### What next?

Below is a list of useful websites relating to this project:
**Picture House**
www.picturehousebelsay.co.uk
**Golan Levin** www.flong.com
**Adam Somlai-Fischer and Bengt Sjölén** www.aether.hu/aleph
**United Visual Artists (UVA)**
www.uva.co.uk
**Pixelache (festival for electronic art and subcultures)**
www.pixelache.ac

For more information, go to www.dott07.com/go/picturehouse

PHOTOS: C – designed by The Roundhouse, photography by John Donoghue

# What makes you feel welcome – or unwelcome?

**Wouldn't it be great if...** unwelcoming experiences could be redesigned?

*'The Welcomes project is about ways to change how we work together, how we live together, how our communities look and feel'*

Stella Hall, Creative Director, culture[10]

## How to be welcoming

A sign at Heathrow's Terminal 4 greets visitors with the words: 'Welcome to Great Britain'. Expectant visitors go through the doors and enter... a grotty gift shop.

Can the North East do better? How might we improve the terminals, ports, places, situations and experiences that greet visitors when they arrive?

The Welcomes project helps communities collect thoughts, ideas and experiences on what makes people feel welcome – or not. They then explore design ideas of ways to make a place more welcoming. Small groups present their ideas as images (drawn, photographed or filmed), written statements and short films.

Welcomes already created range from large-scale set-piece events to one-minute dances, from edible gifts to short films. Each one is designed to celebrate the unique spirit of a city, town or region and reflect the range of cultures now present in the region.

## How did Welcomes work?

Two Welcomes projects were specially commissioned for Dott 07. In Tees Valley, individuals and communities were brought together by independent media company Media 19 to make images, films and audio/written

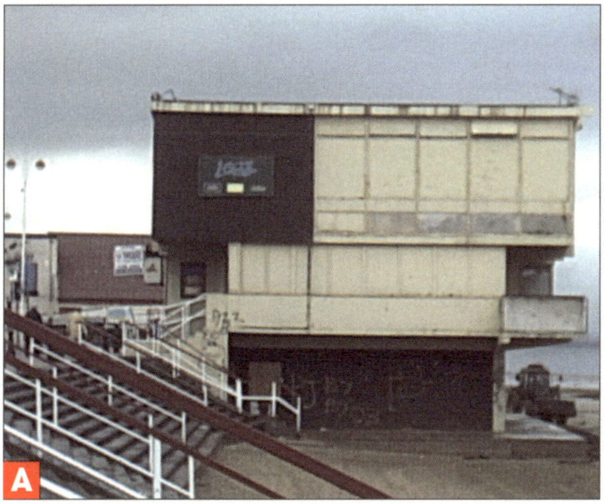


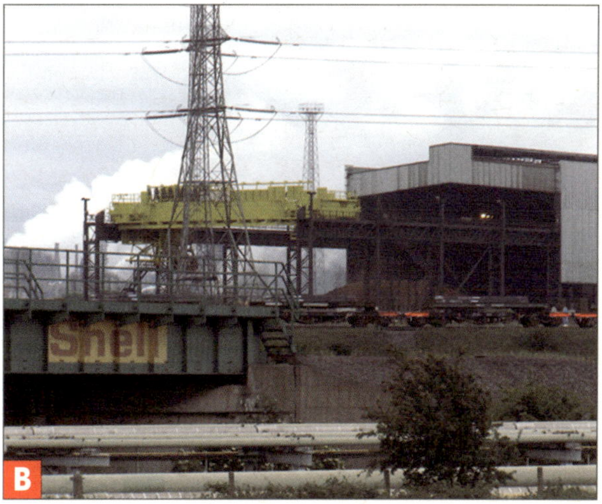


A: 'This is Leo's nightclub. It's what people see when they come to Redcar beaches. It's a horrible, square, unwelcoming 1960s building stuck in the middle of something so beautiful. They should knock this down and turn it into a nice little café.' – Ann Whitham, Tees Valley Housing, Housing Association Panel
B: 'This is the industry near where I live. A lot of people think this is horrible and find it unwelcoming. But it makes me feel at home because I have grown up with it. It gives the area character and, if it all went, I don't know what Middlesbrough would be about.' – Anthony Cornwall, Football First

material. A selection focused on Stockton and Middlesbrough was presented at an exhibition at the Transporter Bridge. An eclectic mix of these short films, photographs, animation clips and written texts was later displayed at the Dott 07 Festival.

Stella Hall, Creative Director, culture[10], who leads the Welcomes project, said the idea is that 'voices will be heard – not just listened to – by the people who make changes'.

Another Welcomes group comprised players and management from Middlesbrough Football Club. Manager Gareth Southgate and first team players Jonathan Woodgate, Jason Euell, Brad Jones, Lee Cattermole and Adam Johnson all contributed to discussions about the welcome they receive from supporters both home and away.

In Stockton, the Sure Start team at Port Clarence Community Centre worked with mums and young children to develop the design for a new park in the heart of their community.

Belinda Williams of Media 19, who helped the group use digital imaging, said: 'The mums here feel isolated because they have to leave their community for most things. They want a park and we want to empower them to get funding. The Welcomes project has raised awareness of what could make Port Clarence a more welcoming place.'

The Berwick on Tweed Welcomes, The Changing Face, celebrates Berwick's young people. It's an alternative to images of its past and

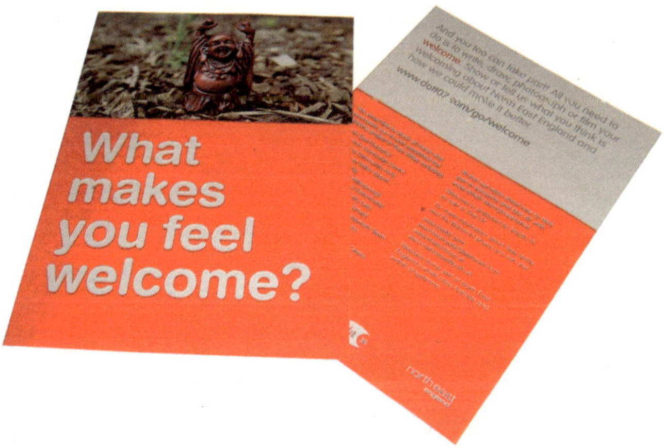


PHOTOS: Welcomes Project / iMedia 19

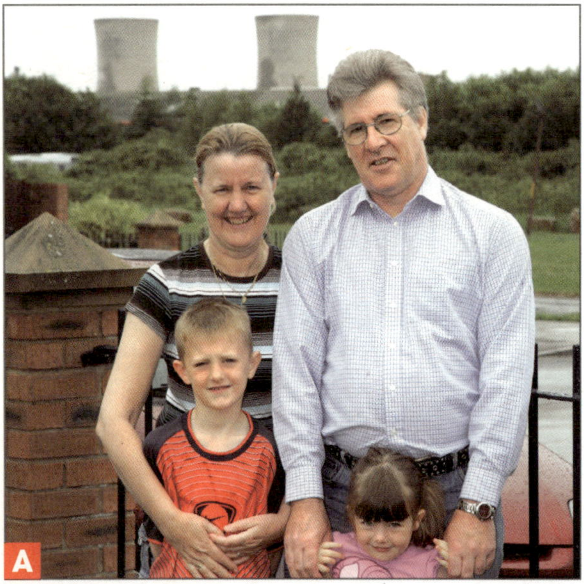

A

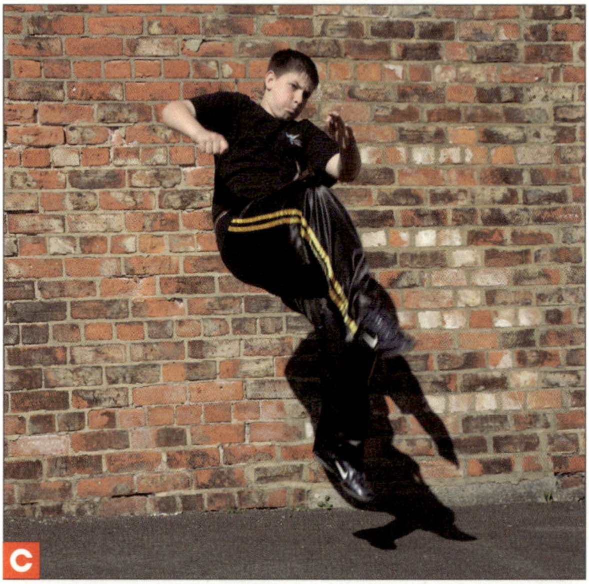

C

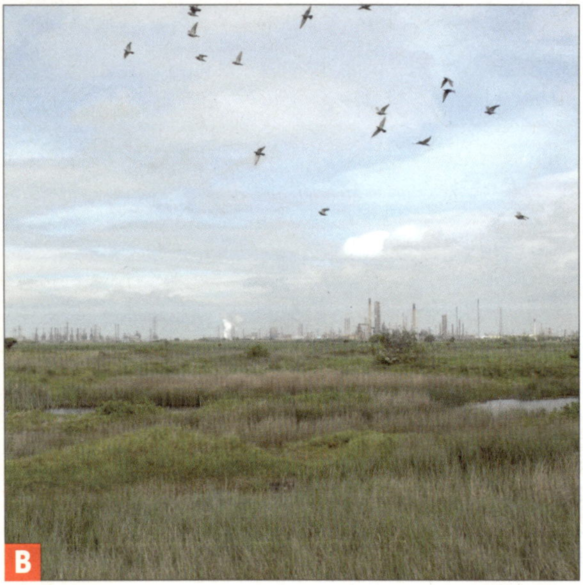

B

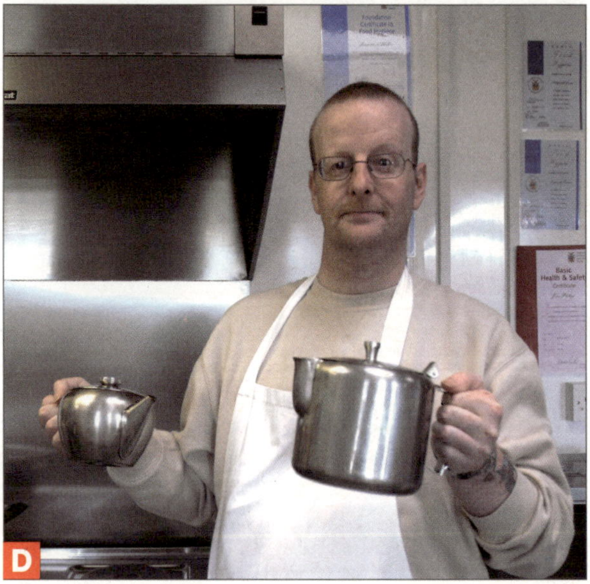

D

PHOTOS: Welcomes Project / Media 19

A: 'Most people think the chimneys are ugly but we love them. They represent our heritage. Industry is what we have grown up with. It is what we are.' – Jim and Val Scollen, Tees Valley Housing, Housing Association Panel
B: 'This is the main field behind the Clarences. It was my playground when I grew up and now it's my little oasis. I would like to see proper paths so the community can benefit from its beauty.' – Jayne Hall, Clarences Community Centre
C: 'I do martial arts so I can defend myself in situations where I might feel unwelcome. When I'm older, being a Black Belt will give me confidence.' – Charlie Hope-Smith, Newtown Community Resource Centre
D: 'To me, the environment or design of a place doesn't make the welcome, it's the people that make the welcome. I always make myself as welcoming as possible.' – Jeff Reynolds, Hemlington Community Café

heritage that normally greet visitors to this picturesque town.

More than 200 young people aged between 14 and 18 helped create a large-scale outdoor projection at the crossing of the town's three famous bridges that, with the River Tweed, mark the boundary between England and Scotland.

A dramatic series of morphing portraits and text, suspended under the central arch of the Royal Tweed Bridge, created a double mirror image of Berwick's collective 'face' through its reflection in the river below.

This project formed part of North East England's world-class festival and events programme.

## What next?

The Welcomes project was the first of its kind. People in the North East were invited to explore what was welcoming or not about their region and to submit their ideas for public display. The best ideas were showcased at the Dott 07 Festival, where visitors could also take part by presenting their Welcomes ideas up until the end of the event.

But the team is determined that the ideas generated have a life beyond the past year's events and directly improve the life of the region and the lives of the community groups that have taken part.

At present, plans to extend the Welcomes project to Stockton and Middlesbrough include a celebration of the Transporter Bridge at its centenary in 2011 and others will be developed across the North East.

For more information about this project, visit:
www.dott07.com/go/welcome
www.media19.co.uk

For opportunities to volunteer at any of the proposed events, visit:
www.visitnewcastlegateshead.com/culture10

If you would like to enquire about usage of the films from the Welcomes event at Berwick or the Transporter Bridge, please contact culture10@ngi.org.uk

If you would like to find out more about this project or to register your interest in the methodology used, please contact Belinda Williams at belinda@media19.co.uk

# Mapping the Necklace: could we build parks without roads and railings?

**Wouldn't it be great if…** a park could be created without turning earth or pouring concrete?

Many tourist destinations are filled with interesting features that visitors, or even residents, never hear about. But what about destinations that are parks that don't, as such, exist? Can you roam a park that can't be seen? Can you map something – a trail, a place, a sense – that is short-lived?

The Dott 07 Mapping the Necklace team explored new ways of mapping transient experiences and hidden places in the Durham Necklace Park – an 'ephemeral park' that spans 12 miles of stunning River Wear-linked pathways.

Developing new recording techniques, they helped bring the Necklace Park's many opportunities to life – not by bulldozing land or erecting buildings, but by personal mapping with the lightest of touch.

## How did Mapping the Necklace work?

It all began with a public movement to recapture their countryside by the people of Durham city and its surrounding villages – and their Necklace Park has since become written into Durham Master Plan. Yet surprisingly little mapping information existed about the Necklace Park area, so the Dott 07 Mapping Team, led by senior producer Susan Williamson, encouraged people to explore this 'ephemeral' park's possibilities as a venue for creative work and other activities and create a new network of North Eastern 'mappers'.

Twenty-five mapping teams were formed and their activities covered a

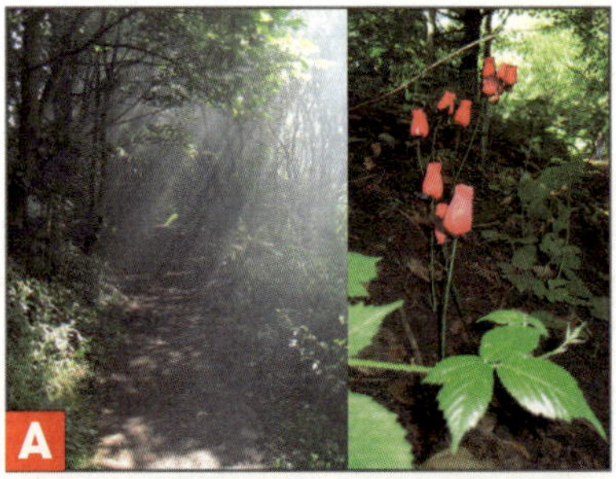

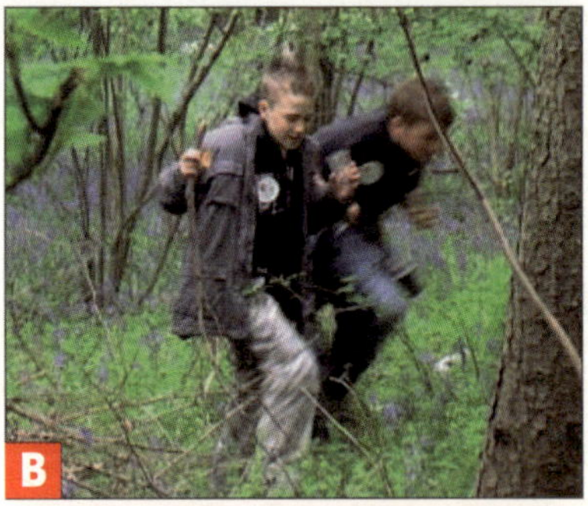

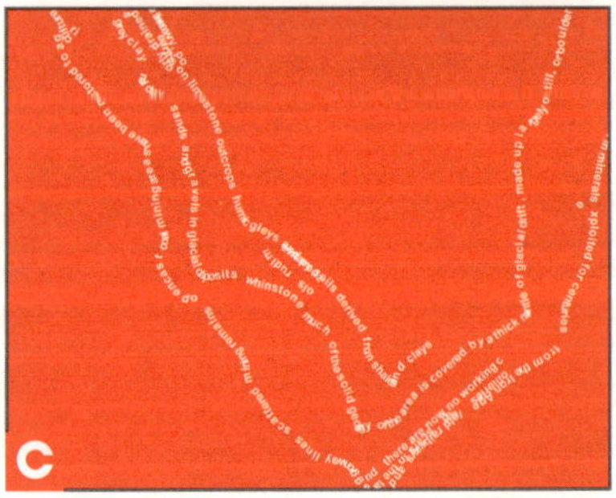

A: Design Camp Snow White Map
B: Play Mappers
C: Chaos Mapping in the Durham Necklace Park

CREDIT: A – Cornerstone Strategies 2007; B – Carcline Kerslake; C – Cipriano Martinez

# Necklace Park... and land identifications

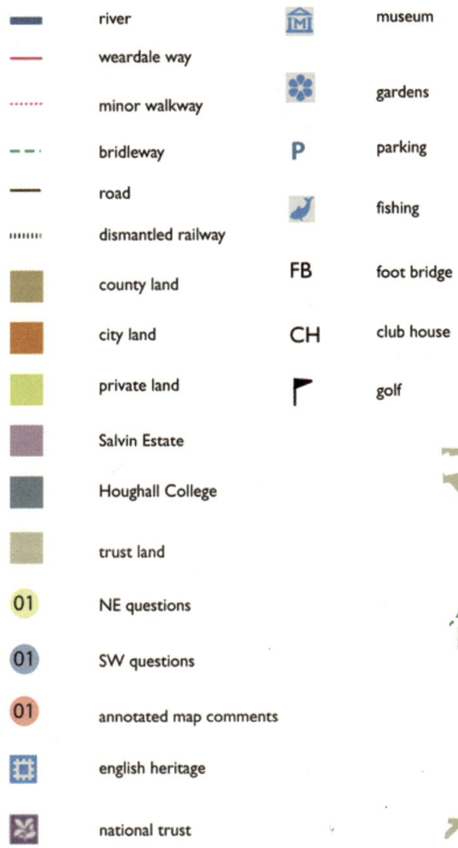


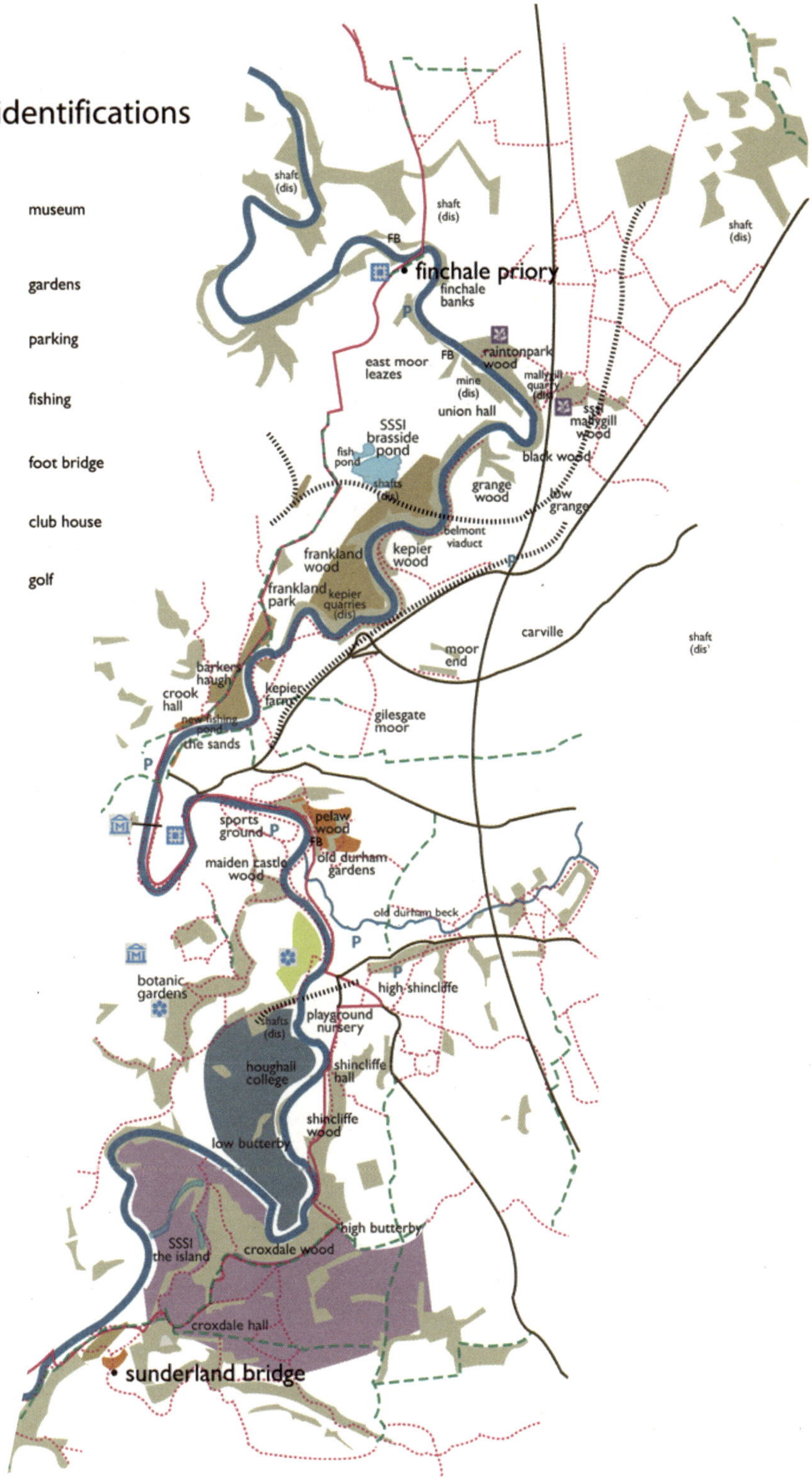


MAP: The Chambers / Cornerstone Strategies 2005

Necklace Park was born when the people of Durham set out to recapture their countryside. The 12-mile (20km) stretch of river is filled with all kinds of treasures – from wild garlic to abandoned coal mines. But many of these features were hard to find, inaccessible, or simply not known about.

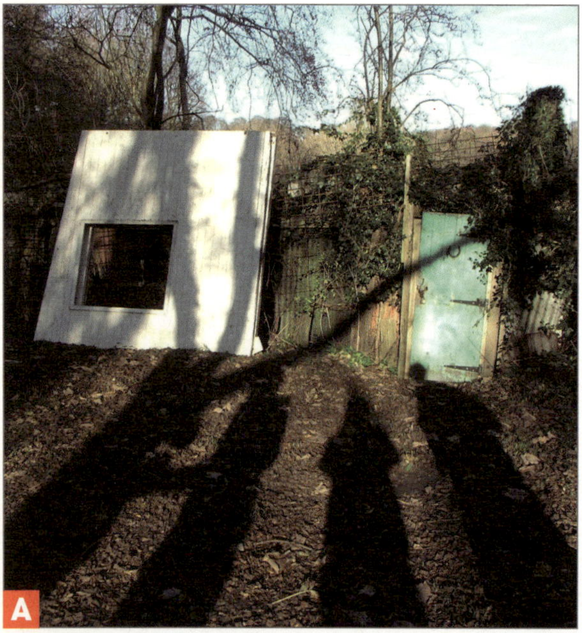


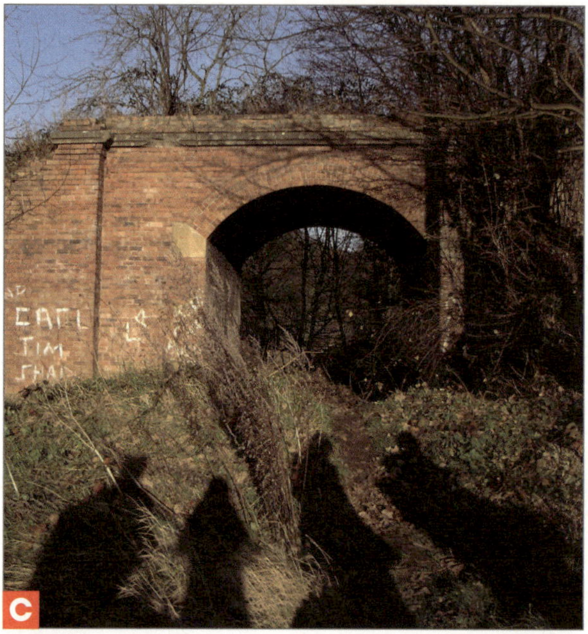


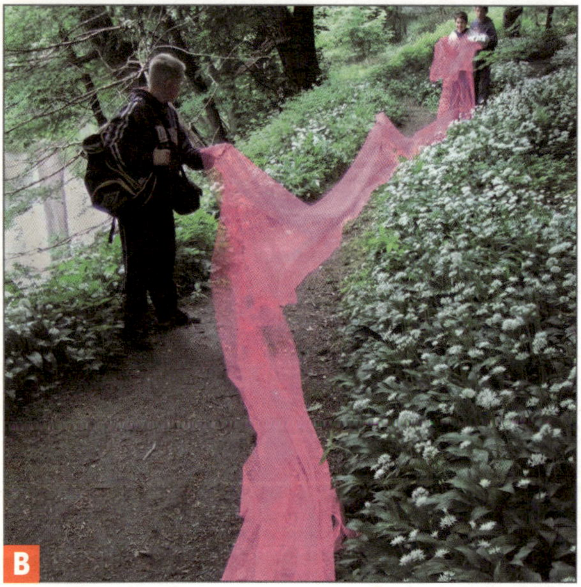


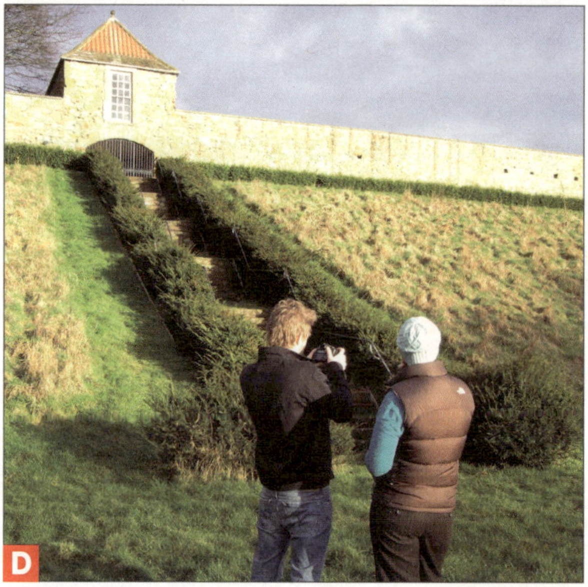


A: Shelter Mapping
B: Mapping Belmont Viaduct

C: Readers of the Lost Art – graphic novelists doing site research
D: Disorienteering team plan mapping packs

CREDIT: Cornerstone Strategies 2007

wide range of interests. Below is a selection of their work:

- Bird Box Boys – award-winning architects DMSR returned to Durham to map the Belmont Viaduct. They worked with a local school, asking how maps could help make the viaduct more accessible to the public
- Audio Mapping – Durham's Society for the Blind and Partially Sighted mapped the park as an audio soundtrack, using ambient sounds and verbal cues as markers
- Readers of the Lost Art – a group of comic-book enthusiasts created stories based on historical information about the park and made their own comic
- Access – two wheelchair users tested the park's accessibility and mapped their findings
- Disorienteering – this team explored the idea that every spot has a different significance for each visitor: one person's ordinary playground swing is the site of another's first kiss. The team asked residents to reflect on aspects of their lives in the park, then helped them map the unexpected interpretations of everyday places.

## What is mapping?

'Mapping' is simply recording your presence in a place. It can be done with a picture, a pen and paper, a video or anything you can get your hands on. For example, if you took a photo of yourself on your mobile phone, or wrote a poem about how you feel, then text it or email it to a friend – that would be an example of mapping. We map our lives every day.

'Mapping is about the interaction between people and a place and being able to share that. People are unfamiliar with [the concept of] mapping and maps, but we do it quite naturally. For example, we have a mental map of the supermarket where we might skip certain aisles.' – Becky Dodds, Mapping the Necklace team

This project formed part of North East England's world-class festival events programme.

**Some examples of Mapping the Necklace:**

- Recording a journey by you, by others, by your ancestors, by wildlife
- Recording a trail you want others to follow – from wild garlic to abandoned mines
- Recording a performance or a sport that uses the park as a venue
- Recording sounds, sights and stories that evoke the Necklace Park
- Recording journeys of reality and guidance, fantasy and speculation

## What next?

You too can start mapping now! At its simplest, mapping is recording your presence in a place, which is exactly what Mapping the Necklace was all about. In Durham, some mappers have formed community action groups.

Mapping tools are available on the Mapping the Necklace website, where you can get involved in the Necklace Park and 'meet' other people like yourself.

In the long term, the Necklace Park is written into the Durham Vision until 2020. It's seen by the city as a key way to improve the Durham experience for residents and visitors alike.

If you would like to find out more about this project, please contact Claire Lancaster or Becky Dodds on +44 191 3833041 or visit **www.durhamnecklacepark.org.uk** or **www.dott07.com**

Other recommended websites:
**www.mapping-the-necklace.org.uk**
**www.durhamvision.org.uk**
**www.cornerstonestrategies.co.uk**

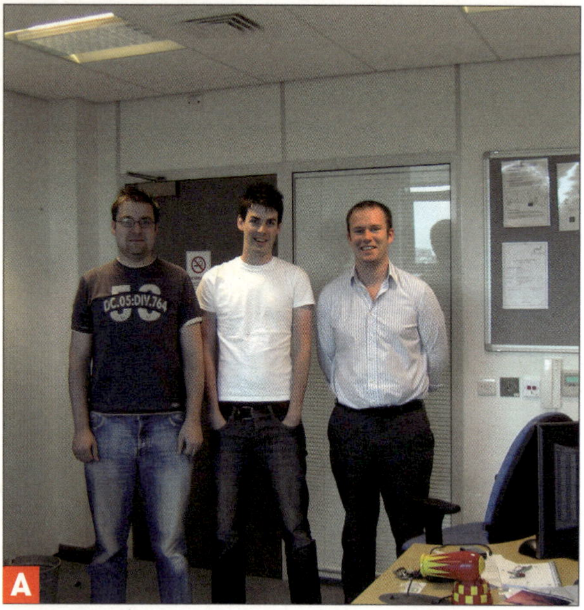

A

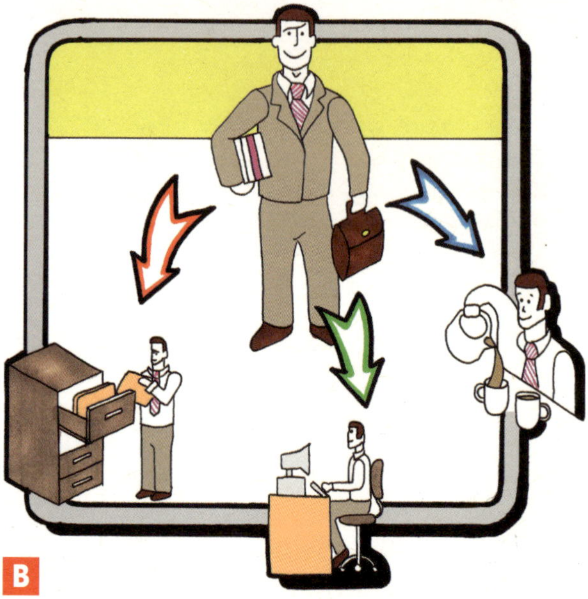

B

# New Work: how do *you* want to work?

**Wouldn't it be great if...** working people helped each other out more with the practical hassles that wear us down?

## 88% of people in the North East work for, or as, a business with four people or less[8]

## Lack of social interaction is as much of a challenge as lack of work

### What this has got to do with movement?

Remember all those books and reports about 'the future of work'? Well, the future seems to have arrived. A report from Orange called *The way to work*[9] states that 55% of the UK workforce does not have a job in the traditional sense of the word. And a lot of our working lives is spent moving around.

Dott 07's New Work project is about practical design steps to improve the day-to-day experience of people who are self-employed or have a micro-business. Many people who work from home complain that they often feel isolated, and would like to exchange skills and services with each other on a local basis. They also need help accessing the 300 or more government assistance schemes. Helping working people meet each other on a local basis has emerged as another key feature.

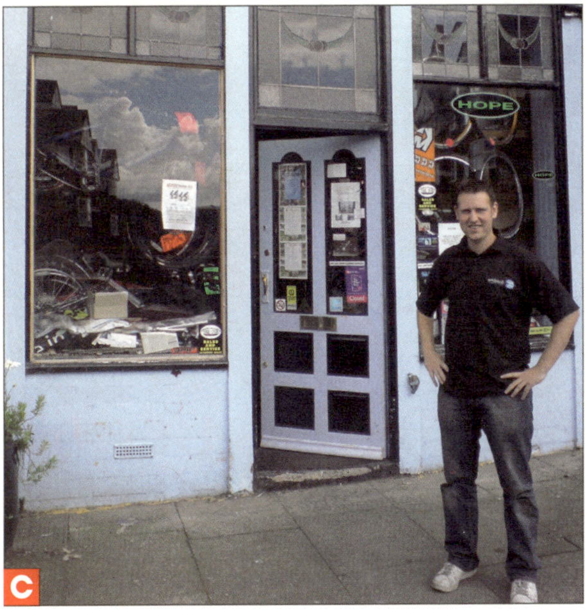


C

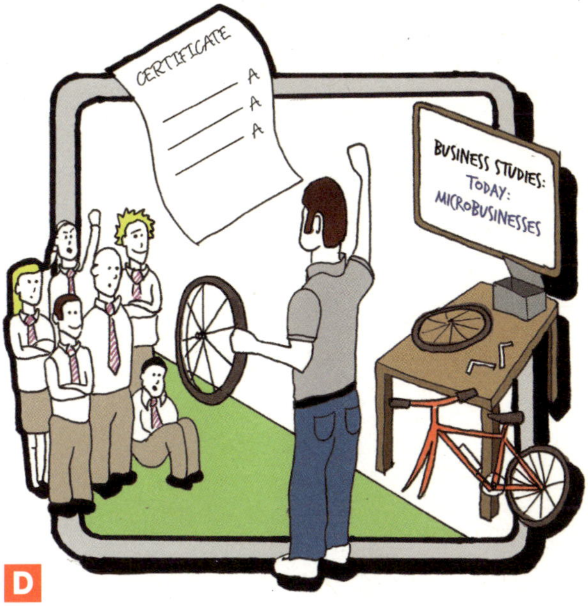


D

## How did New Work work?

Many designers are already involved in the creation of hardware for work: desks, lights, chairs and so on. But with numbers of self-employed people set to rocket nationwide, our next challenge is to redesign the how, where and when of work. With this in mind, New Work asked the question 'How do you design your life?' and looked at the specific problems facing this rapidly increasing section of the workforce.

Project management company Enabling Concepts chose six diverse small business owners at different stages of growth to take part in a case-study programme. With the help of service designers live|work, they met regularly and identified what they each needed to facilitate being the boss of a successful micro-business.

The workshops revealed six top issues of concern for those running a micro-business:

- Both finding the right staff and keeping them
- Selling products and services
- Delegating responsibility to others
- Keeping up standards when expanding
- Accessing finance and investment
- Managing time effectively

Ideas from their discussions were developed into services to respond to each of the problems identified. Enabling Concepts then guided the businesses in how they might deliver those services collaboratively.

The case-study group went on to create an online forum open to the public to pilot the new services with each other and their growing network.

This ever-expanding group of micro-businesses continues to meet online and in person, and an increasing number of services continue to be delivered to them as well as to any other interested micro-businesses.

**A&B:** Challenge: the different skills we need
*'I have a sales role, an investment role, a toned-down coding role… hell, I even change the toilet roll' Ross, Rozmic*
Service design idea: share the right person – a skilled person is shared by two or more businesses

**C&D:** Challenge: social isolation
*'My work is my passion and I'd love to share my enthusiasm with others' Ben, Whiptail Cycles*
Service design idea: working back at school – micro-business runs an in-school workshop. The students learn about your business, and you get to interact with young people in the local community

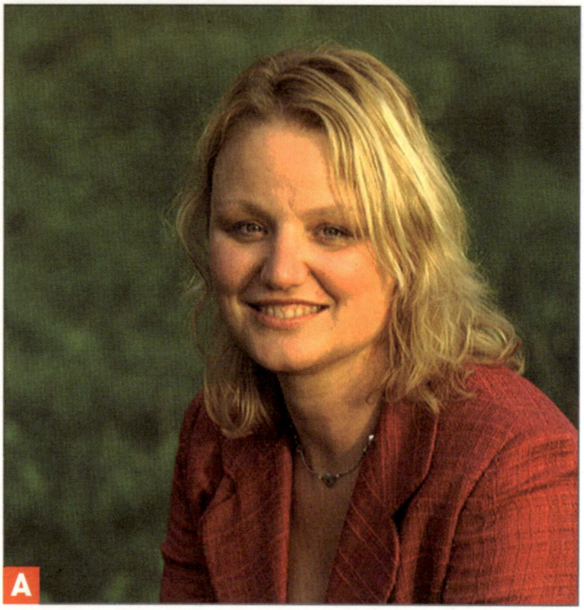

A

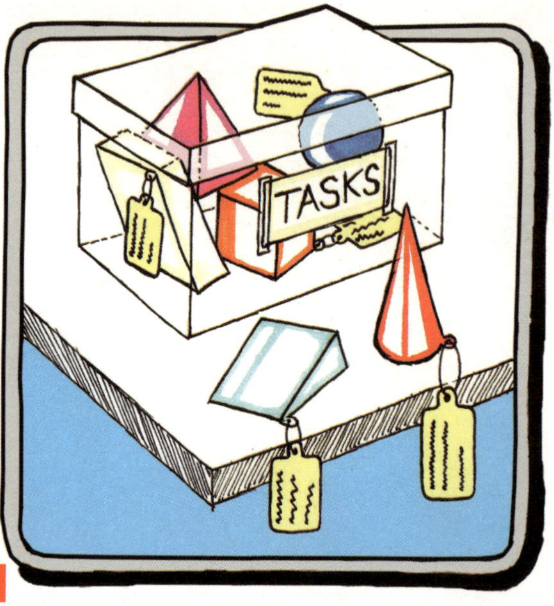


B

## *Who is the happiest of them all?*

*According to the City & Guilds Happiness Index[10], hairdressers are the happiest workers in Britain: 40% say they are very content in their job (giving their careers a score of 10 out of 10). Next in the happiness stakes are the clergy (24%), chefs/cooks (23%), beauticians (22%) and plumbers, mechanics and builders (all 20%). In contrast, only 5% of lawyers, IT specialists and secretaries/PAs, 4% of estate agents, 3% of civil servants and 2% of architects say they are extremely happy at work. Even that score seems doomed to plummet once architects hear the City & Guilds advice on how to achieve happiness in the workplace: 'Enrich your working environment with photos and flowers'.*

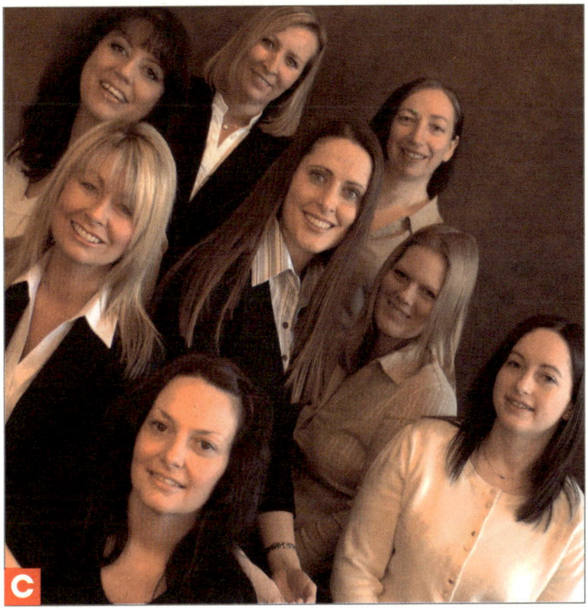

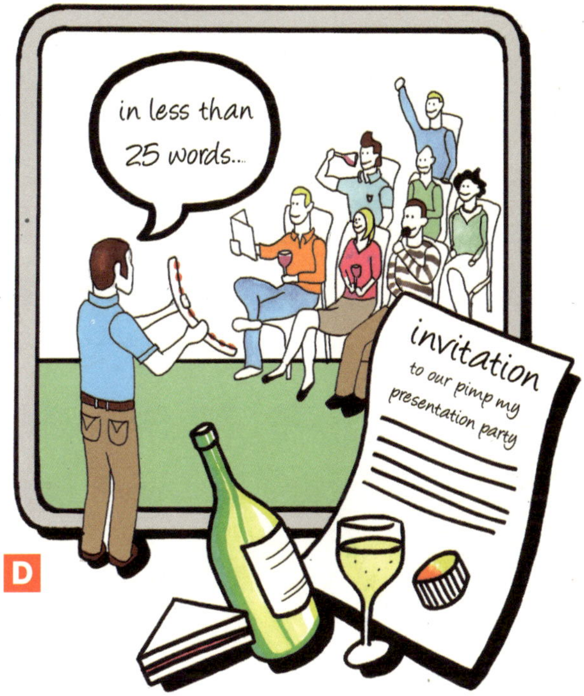


**A&B:** Challenge: time pressure
*'I had a few days off a while ago – but all I did was worry whether the business would cope without me' – Manuela, Lexica Communications*
Service design idea: 'Get it done' game – turn 'to do' lists into a game, use objects to represent tasks, then give the objects to others. This helps keep track of tasks and gets them done on time

**C&D:** Challenge: giving presentations
*'We need to improve the presentation we give to potential customers – but we don't have the skills or the time' – Fiona, Julie and team, The Wellness Centre*
Service design idea: pimp my presentation – a social event and workshop at which professionals help each other to improve their presentation skills and materials

## What next?

New Work explored issues that challenge people in a wide variety of work situations: time issues; access to tools and skills; feelings of loneliness and social isolation; the need for places to meet and socialise and share.

Below is a list of useful websites related to this project:

**Fabrium Networks – an online forum helping small businesses to exchange services with each other**
www.fabriam.net

**Enabling Concepts**
www.enablingconcepts.co.uk

**Street North East: Financial and business advice for the smallest of businesses**
www.streetnortheast.co.uk

**Selling small amounts of time**
www.nationalmarkets.com/index.html

**Kevin Kelly's Cool Tools**
www.kk.org/cooltools/index.php

**How to stage a speed meeting**
http://people.interaction-ivrea.it/j.tester/speedmeeting/

For more information, contact Nathan Pellow at npellow@enablingconcepts.co.uk or go to www.dott07.com/go/newwork

# Energy: a new approach

Can the North East do for energy what Stephenson's *Rocket* did for transportation?

**Each day, we all contribute to climate change through energy-dependent activities such as driving, heating or cooling our homes, taking flights, disposing of waste – and eating**

Energy is a fundamental requirement of modern life. We rely on it to provide heat and light, to cook, communicate, move around and make things.

Producing the energy required for these activities means burning fossil fuels – oil, coal and gas. This leads to an accumulation of greenhouse gases in the atmosphere, a process that slowly heats up the planet and leads to global warming. More and more people, aware of the dangers of climate change, want to take action.

Renewable energy technologies are becoming more important at a local, national and global level. Most renewable energy comes from the heat and light of the sun (wind, solar, wave, biomass). Other renewable energy comes from the gravitational pull of the moon (lunar power) and the sun on the oceans (tidal) and from the hot rocks found deep within the earth (geothermal). The primary advantage of renewable energy is that it does not produce the gases that are associated with climate change. And renewable forms of energy will not run out.

## What is the North East doing for energy?

The North East has important market-leading expertise in a variety of new and renewable energy solutions. The region's wind- and sea-based energy systems are developed at Blyth's Centre for New and Renewable Energy. A variety of land-based energy systems – hydro, solar, biomass and wind micro-generation – are also being developed. Fuel cells are being developed at the Centre for Process Innovation, biomass systems at Cockle Farm, and next-generation photovoltaics at Durham University. In the public domain, a £20million project called

The Watershed will be a unique renewable energy model village in a former cement works.

## How Dott 07 helped

Dott 07's Low Carb Lane project (pages 44-47) sought to create user-friendly visualisations of energy use (based on a real-life case study) and make them a starting point from which to develop a practical prototype for sustainable household energy use.

The North East Energy Futures images (pages 48-51) depict what new and renewable energy technologies could look like if they were to be deployed in the North East in the coming years. In place of today's coal-fired power stations, we will see geothermal extraction rigs, biomass boilers and lunar energy in the form of micro-hydro installations that harness the power of the tides.

**How energy is used in the UK**

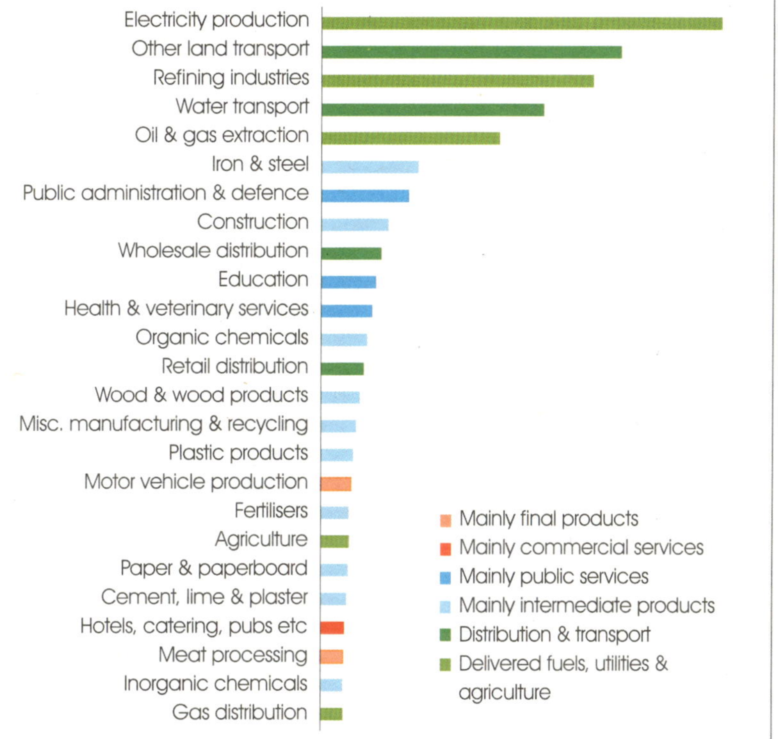


BAR CHART: Carbon Trust (www.carbontrust.co.uk)

### Future Currents

One third of the UK's greenhouse gas emissions come from residential households[11]. Householders could reduce this by making their houses more efficient, generating their own energy, switching suppliers or simply switching off. But power bills are confusing, energy use is invisible and alternative installations are tedious to procure, often expensive and hard to maintain.

The RED team at the Design Council in London experienced these frustrations first-hand while living in a terraced house in London. Their Future Currents project proposed new products, services and policies to help householders save energy and reduce the $CO_2$ emissions they produce. Proposals included devices for home monitoring and regulatory schemes to rank and reward citizens for good energy behaviour. Find out more at: **www.designcouncil.info/futurecurrents/**

# Low Carb Lane: how can we pay less for warmer homes?

**Wouldn't it be great if...** energy efficiency was the easy option?

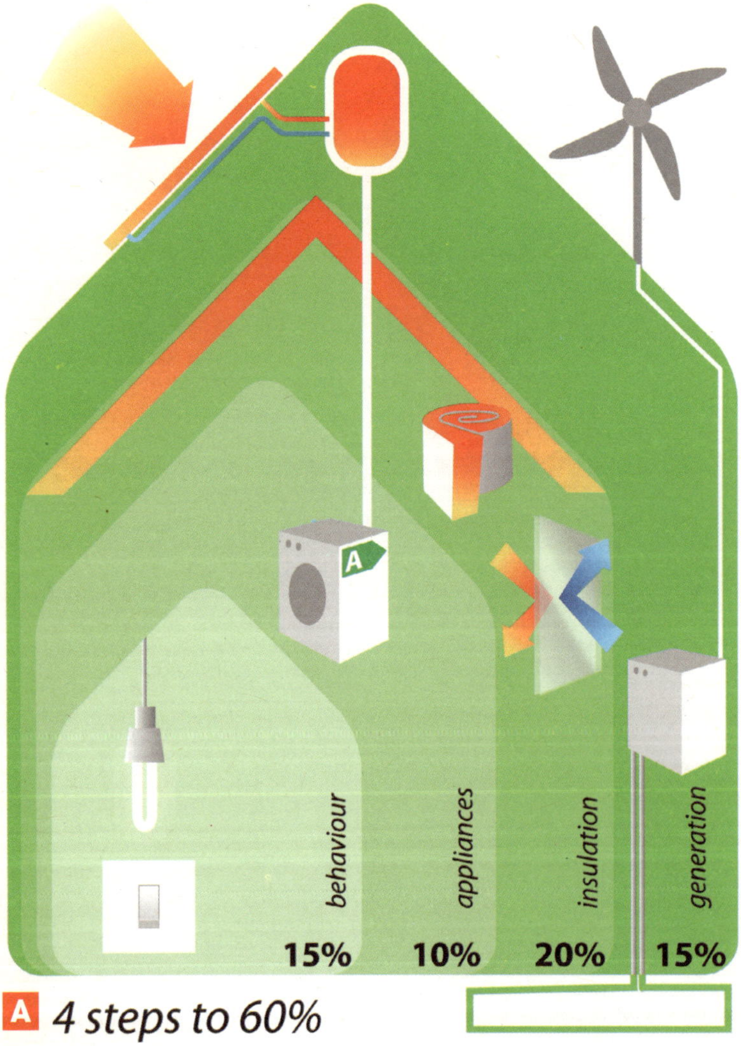


**A** *4 steps to 60%*

## The home energy challenge

Many of us would like to reduce the greenhouse gas emissions from our energy use at home. Other people have different priorities. What we have in common is the desire to reduce our energy bills. How might energy efficiency be accessible, desirable and affordable for all – rich or poor, home owners and renters alike?

## How did Low Carb Lane work?

Dott's Low Carb Lane team, led by Ben Reason and Alex Webb Allen, spent more than a year with the community at Castle Terrace. We learned about the social and economic situation of citizens affected by fuel poverty. The team then created a way to visualise energy use using a television-based 'home energy dashboard', which enables the occupier to understand where their energy is used and so control it better. They then developed a 'pay-as-you-save' scheme called SaverBox, which removes financial barriers to investing in energy-efficient home improvements.

During our time in Low Carb Lane, we learned that there are many issues surrounding energy efficiency and a variety of barriers in the way of change. The residents' main concern was the decline of the street, both physically and in terms of the

**A: live|work's graphic shows how small changes in our homes and behaviour could more than halve our energy use**

ILLUSTRATIONS/PHOTO: live|work

community spirit. These issues far outweighed climate change and personal energy consumption.

The street is split 50/50 between owner-occupiers and tenants of private rental properties. Many of the owner-occupiers blame the decline of the community on the rise in privately rented properties. Some landlords, they say, do not invest in their properties and allow them to fall into disrepair. This results in a general decline in the physical appearance of the street as a whole. Homeowners are then less inclined to invest in their own properties, something that is beyond the financial means of many residents to begin with. These issues explain why there is apathy towards climate change.

The introduction of the energy dashboard was motivated by the suggestion by some researchers that real-time feedback raises awareness and enables people to budget.

We also looked at practical changes to the products, appliances and interiors we use. We made energy savings by choosing certain products over others, from low-cost changes (light bulbs, draught excluders, curtains) to larger investments (such as A-rated white goods and boilers). We also investigated how insulating homes can significantly reduce energy consumption and generate large savings on energy bills.

We also looked at off-grid power generation – introducing solar thermal system, explaining why we chose it, and giving an objective presentation of all the pros and cons of various renewable energy technologies.

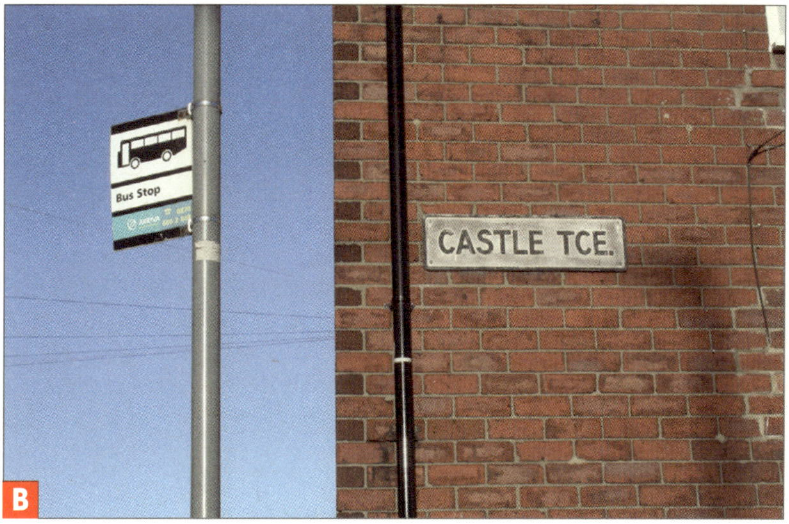


B: Castle Terrace, the location of Low Carb Lane

**In Denmark, almost 60% of heating needs are met by district heating[12]**

**Home energy dashboard**

The Low Carb Lane TV-based home energy dashboard communicates the relative savings of all the above and was displayed at the Dott 07 Festival.

With energy being an invisible entity, the only points of reference for the amount of energy we use are our utility bills. These are often complicated and many people feel they lack control over their energy spend due to a lack of transparent information.

The Low Carb Lane project was informed by several metering projects that live|work has been involved in, the most recent being a Swedish Energy Agency-funded research project called WATTCH. This explored the potential for 'smart-metering' technology (currently being rolled out in Sweden and the Netherlands) to provide clear real-time energy consumption information, in the form of a screen-based 'energy dashboard' to domestic users via their televisions, computers and mobile phones.

The WATTCH dashboard not only provided this information to empower the domestic energy consumer and raise awareness of energy use, it also proposed a reward scheme to encourage further efficiency and influence our energy behaviour.

The WATTCH project resulted in a fully working prototype that was tested in several households in Sweden. It used internet-enabled televisions and computers and received lots of positive feedback. The Low Carb Lane project has been an ideal platform to continue developing the concept, and hopefully bring the dashboard to market in the coming years. WATTCH this space!

**SaverBox**

Several people on Castle Terrace said that they'd love to cut their energy bills by 50%, but didn't have the money for the necessary home improvements.

The SaverBox, exhibited at the Dott 07 Festival, was created in response to these concerns. It is a package of energy-saving measures, such as loft and cavity-wall insulation, that make your home both cheaper to run and greener.

The idea is simple: someone either comes round to your house to perform an energy audit, or it can be done over the phone. Suitable SaverBox packages are then offered to the household – SaverBox Loft Insulation, for example.

If the household agrees to the offer, the loft insulation is provided and installed (by qualified installers) at no up-front cost. Then, each month, the household agrees to pay off the cost of the loft insulation at a rate less than the energy savings generated by the loft insulation. So, the household is paying for the insulation without feeling the financial pinch and saving energy.

Northumberland WarmZones, Ashington Credit Union, National Energy Action and the Wansbeck LIFE Initiative are involved in the SaverBox scheme. live|work hopes to replicate the scheme nationwide using the existing structure of credit unions.

**NESCO**

It can be difficult to know how much energy you are using and how much it will cost, so live|work has created NESCO (North East Energy Service Co-operative), a proposed not-for-profit energy utility. It puts its members in control of their energy use and encourages energy efficiency by making energy understandable and the payment processes transparent.

NESCO members receive a fixed monthly payment and accurate real-time information about their energy use, so they can compare their actual use with their monthly payment.

While NESCO buys energy in bulk for cheaper than the market rate, it does not sell it on to its members at this rate as cheaper energy would not encourage energy saving. This profit goes into a pot, which is used to fund NESCO's points scheme. This rewards individual households for saving energy – for example, 'Save £10 of energy this month and get £10 of cinema tickets'.

The reward scheme could also operate on a community-wide level. The 'pot' would also fund the installation of the home energy dashboard to all members' homes, and could also provide the funding basis for communities to access renewable technologies, such as solar thermal systems, heat pumps and wood-chip boiler systems.

Hopefully, helping people to lower their energy bills and rewarding them for doing so will prove popular, and NESCO can be put into practice.

First, however, we will need to test it in a larger community to see whether it can really work.

C

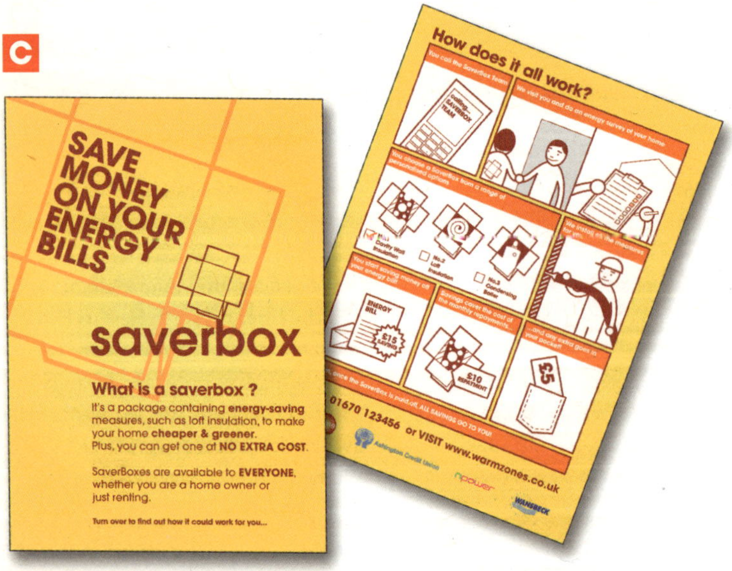

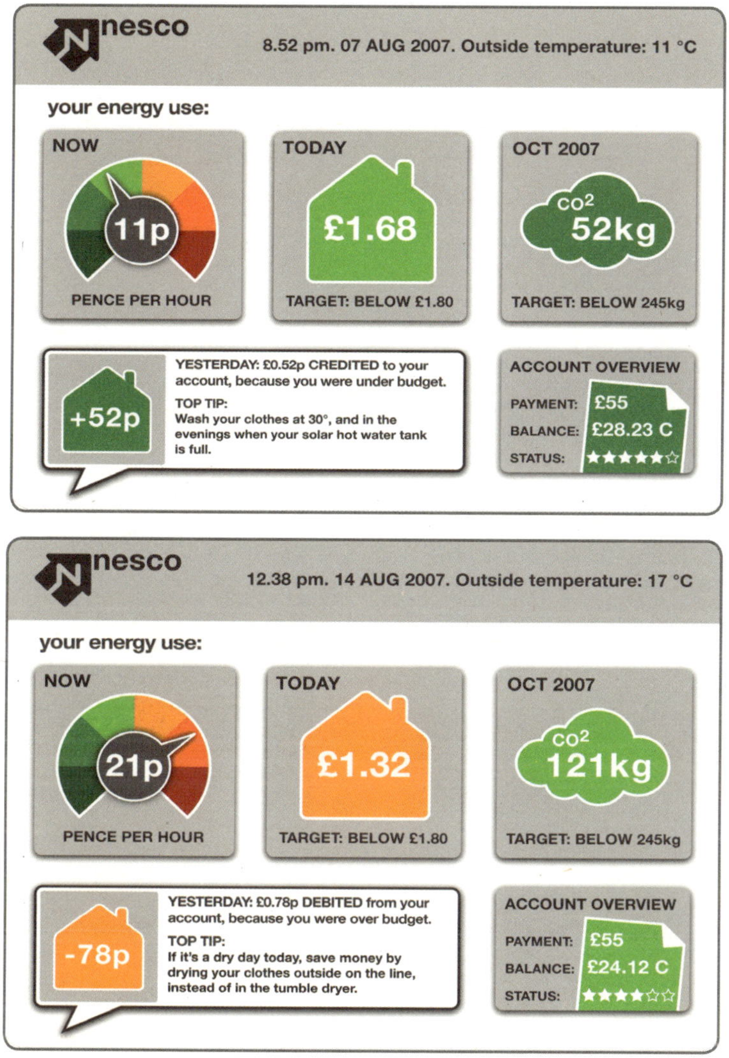


**D**

**C:** the SaverBox is a package of energy-saving measures designed to help households cut their energy bills
**D:** NESCO would use an energy dashboard to show consumers exactly how their energy consumption compares with their bill – and how they could do better

## What next?

Dott's Low Carb Lane team looked for ways to make energy loss visible, and put the information about power use on a domestic dashboard viewed on your TV screen.

So far, so good. The next step was to figure out how such a dashboard might help us change behaviour – not just sit there making us feel anxious. To this end, live|work proposed NESCO which was presented in the Dott Festival. They are now talking to potential partners about trialling the NESCO scheme in community of around 100 houses. The NESCO would act as a local energy supplier, offer energy at flat rates to both credit and pre-pay energy customers, and also offer reward points for energy saving.

Will all this happen? Within a year or so, an interactive extension of the TV dashboard system could enable members of the NESCO to network and communicate to them the potential benefits of energy saving to both individuals and the community through the reward scheme. With that in place, it would encourage investment in the physical environment and foster greater community spirit. Power to the people!

For the latest news, go to: **www.dott07.com/go/energy** or **www.livework.co.uk**

For background information, visit the Energy North East website: **www.energynortheast.net/page/whoswho.cfm**

Low Carb Lane was led by live|work (full credits and details can be found on pages 96 to 99).

# North East Energy Futures

The burning of fossil fuels for energy generation results in the emission of harmful gases such as carbon dioxide, methane and sulphur dioxide. These gases have been acknowledged by the world's leading scientists as key contributors to global climate change.

In order to combat the effects of climate change and ensure the stability of energy supplies, renewable energy technologies are important at a local, national and global level.

Renewable energy will not run out. It comes, mostly, from the heat and light of the sun (wind, solar, wave, biomass) though some comes from the gravitational pull of the moon and the sun on the oceans (tidal) and from the hot rocks found deep within the earth (geothermal). Renewable energy does not produce the gases associated with climate change.

But what would these new energy systems look like once deployed here in the North East? Dott 07 (in partnership with Doors of Perception) commissioned Konstantinos Chalaris to create these images. They show the range of new and renewable energy technologies that could be deployed in the North East in the future in actual locations that would suit them, such as rural, urban and suburban settings as well as rivers and the sea.

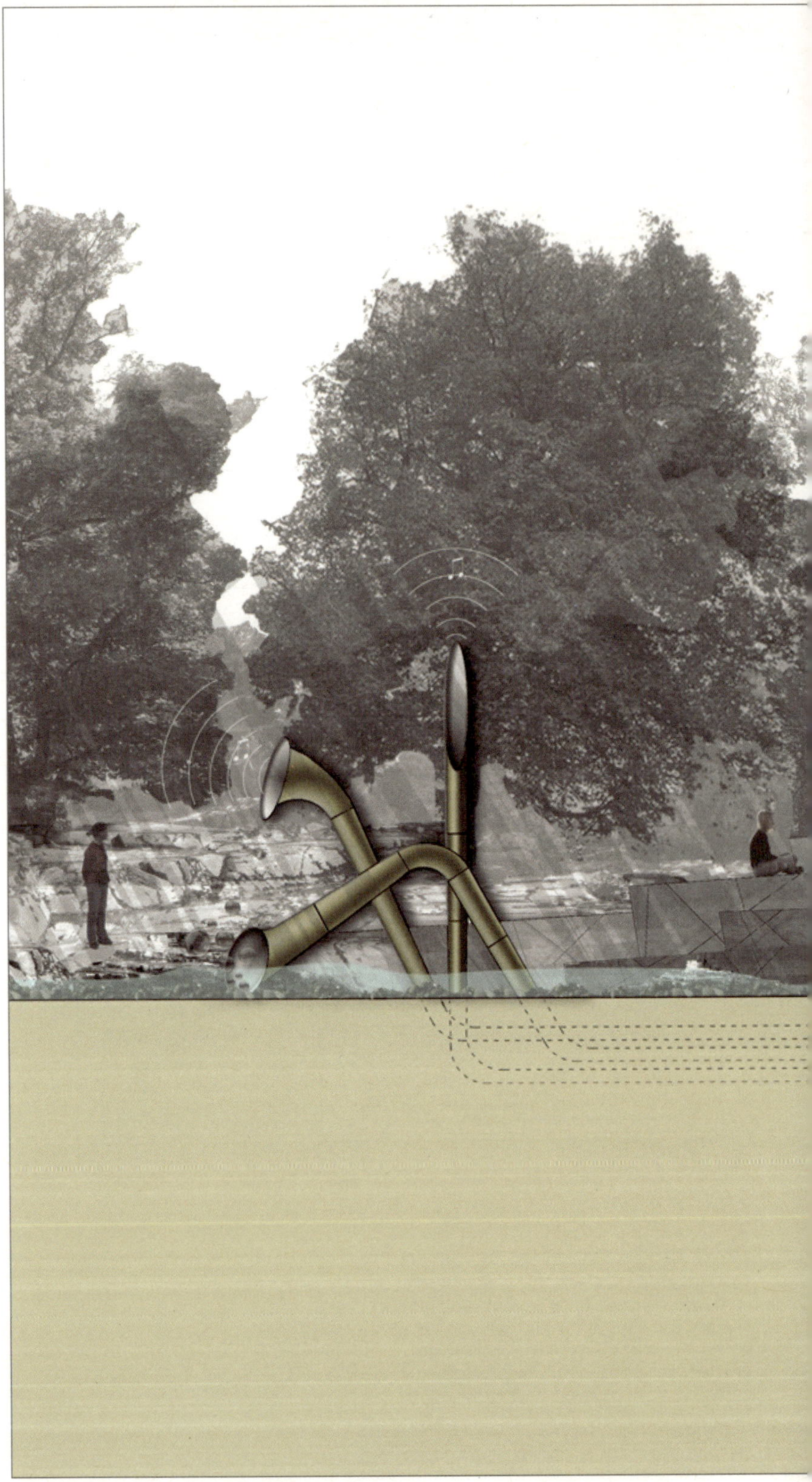

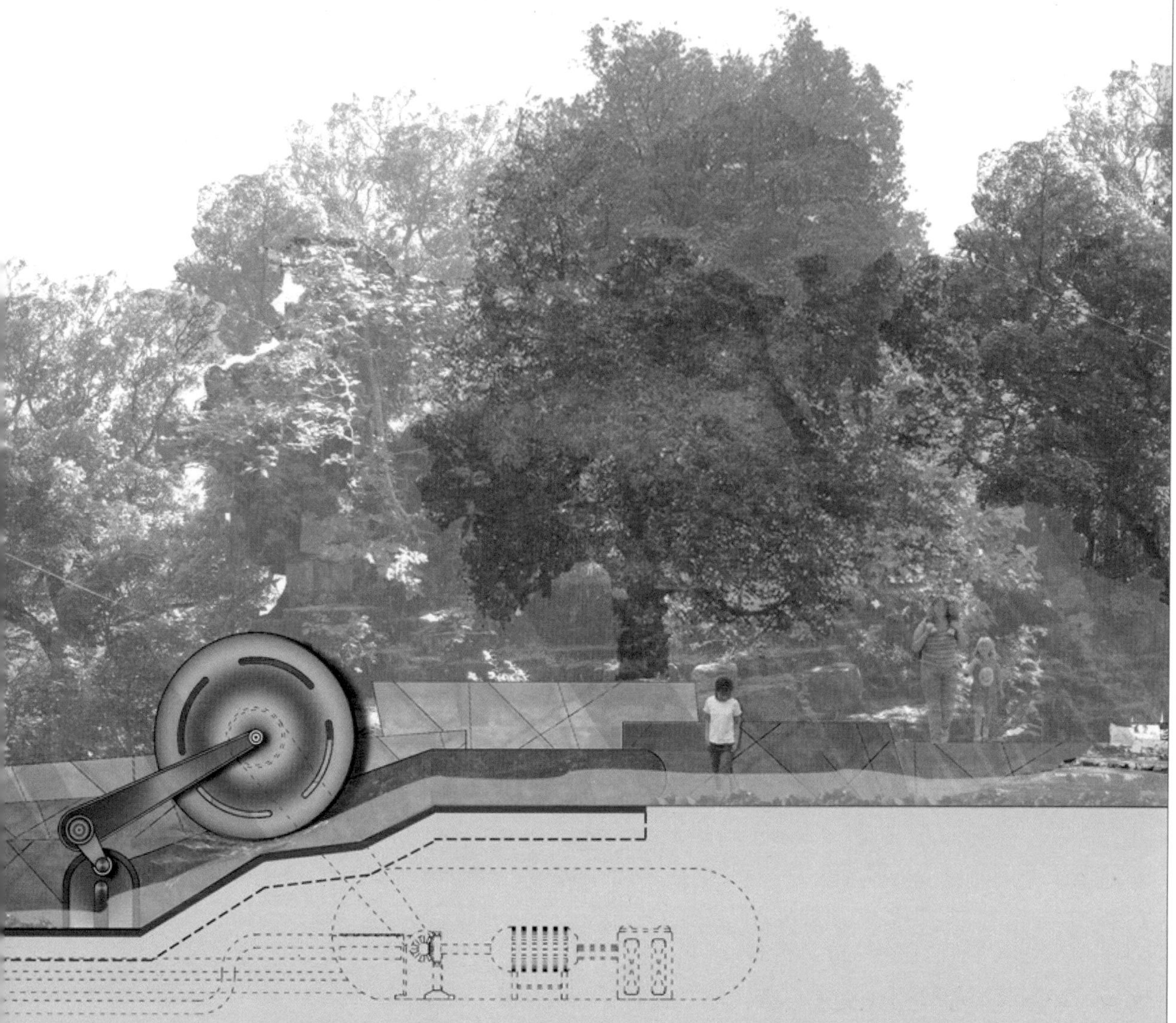

After visiting this small river in Northumberland, Konstantinos Chalaris designed a small scale water mill for energy production. Enchantingly, it also powers a musical instrument that emerges from the water like a water lily. It would produce a gentle musical tone to alert people to the presence of the installaton, which would otherwise remain hidden.

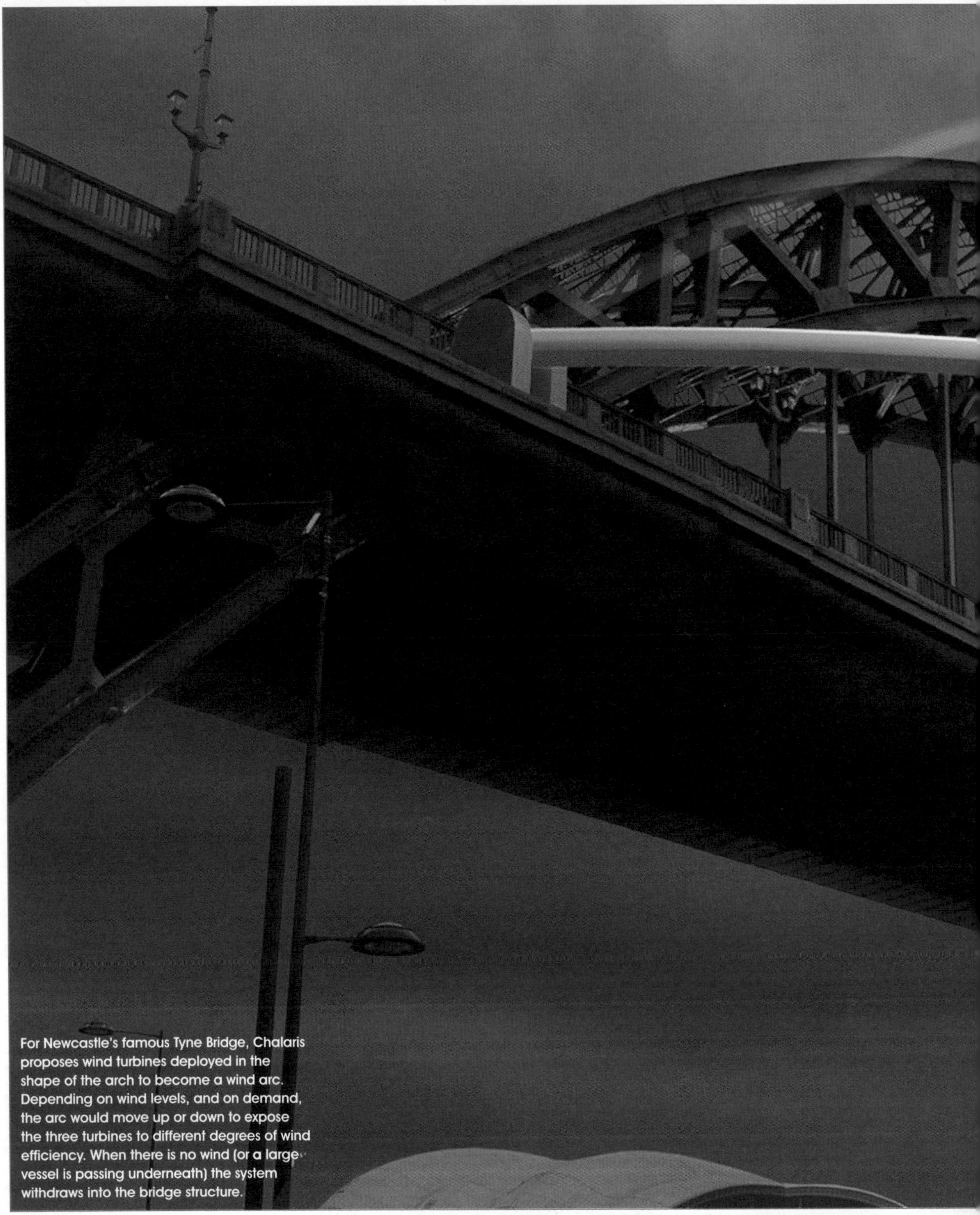

For Newcastle's famous Tyne Bridge, Chalaris proposes wind turbines deployed in the shape of the arch to become a wind arc. Depending on wind levels, and on demand, the arc would move up or down to expose the three turbines to different degrees of wind efficiency. When there is no wind (or a large vessel is passing underneath) the system withdraws into the bridge structure.

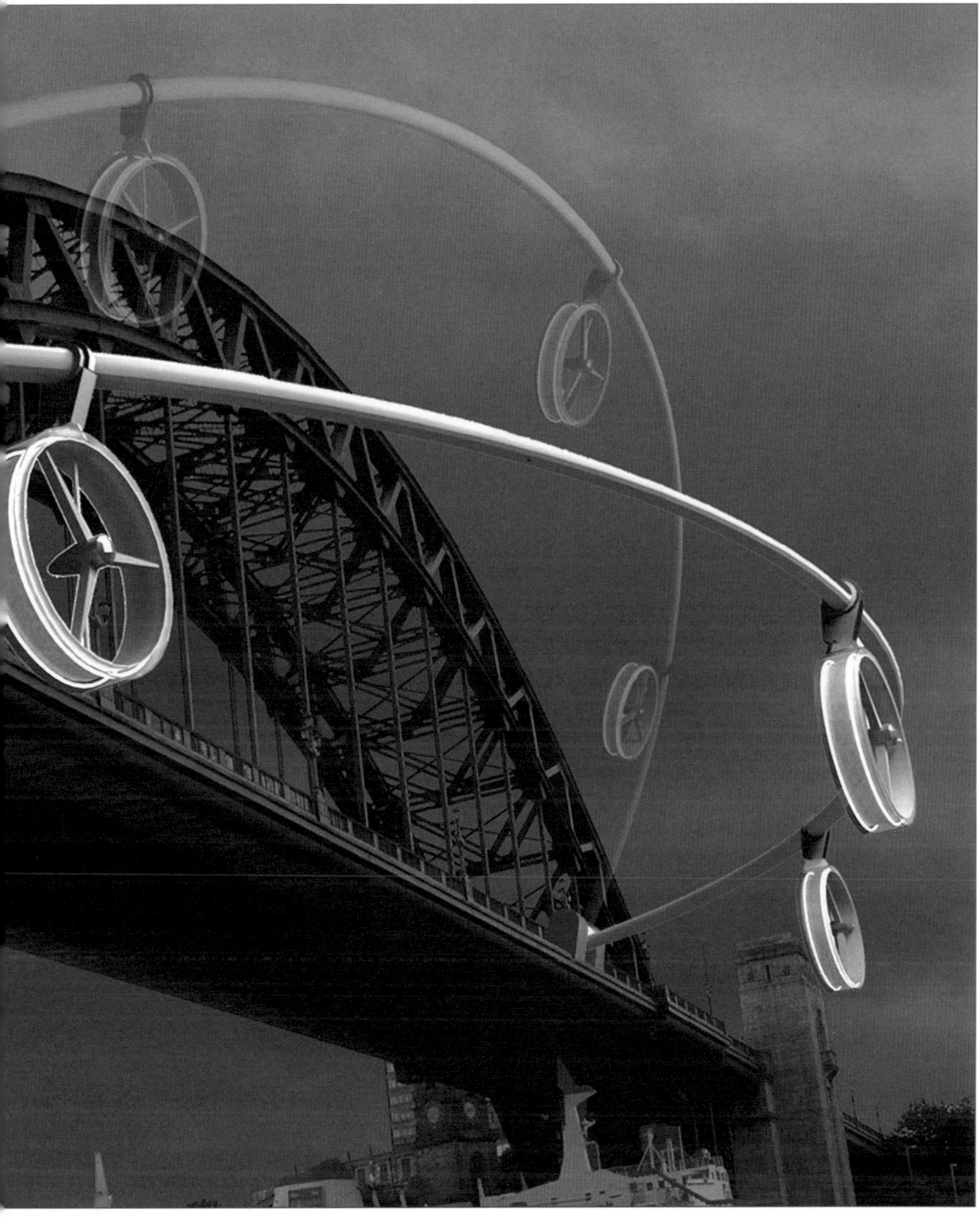

# Schools & schooling: are we giving today's school students enough leeway to shape the world they will live in?

## The school sustainablity challenge

Education lies at the heart of Dott 07. After all, when it comes to sustainability and design, all of us – young and old – need to learn new skills. Dott's objective is to equip the next generation with the insight and skills required to achieve one planet living.

Dott projects support One NorthEast's ambition for people to become expert at finding ways to use science and technology to improve everyday life. They are also aligned with the government's national Sustainable Schools programme, supporting schools on their journey to sustainability, introducing the principles of sustainable development, and offering guidance on how to embed these principles into the heart of school life[13].

In OurNewSchool, Dott 07 asked: 'What are the design priorities when a school is rebuilt?' Dott 07 worked for a year with staff and students in a real school – Walker Technology College – to explore the question via a series of trials and experiments. During the second phase of the project, teachers, parents, students, policymakers and designers debated the lessons they had learned and considered how to reproduce the best experiments on a larger scale. To find out what happens next on schooling and sustainability, read more about this project on pages 60 to 63.

Eco Design Challenge asked Year 8 students across the North East two questions: 'How big is your school's ecological footprint?' and 'What design steps would make it smaller?' We monitored their progress over the year, and you can read about how they fared on pages 54 to 59.

**Below:** schools across the region were challenged and energised by two questions: 'how big is your school's carbon footprint?' and, 'how do you propose to make it smaller?' The Eco Warriors below, created by design firm NE6, featured in the communication campaign for Eco Design Challenge

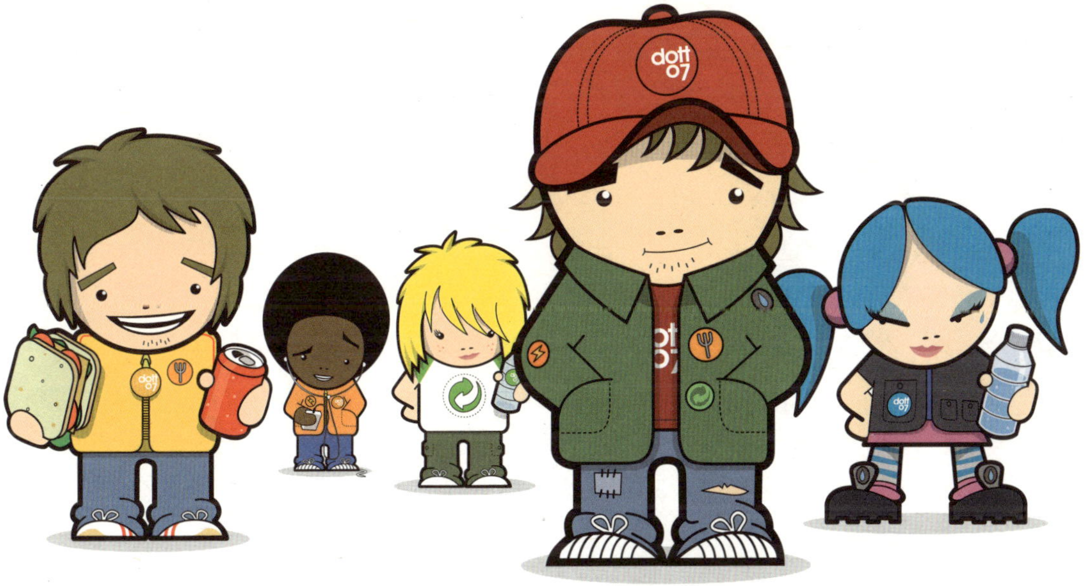


ILLUSTRATION: NE6 Design Consultants Ltd

# Eco Design Challenge: how big is *your* school's ecological footprint?

**Wouldn't it be great if...** we let students take the lead in reducing the eco footprint of their school?

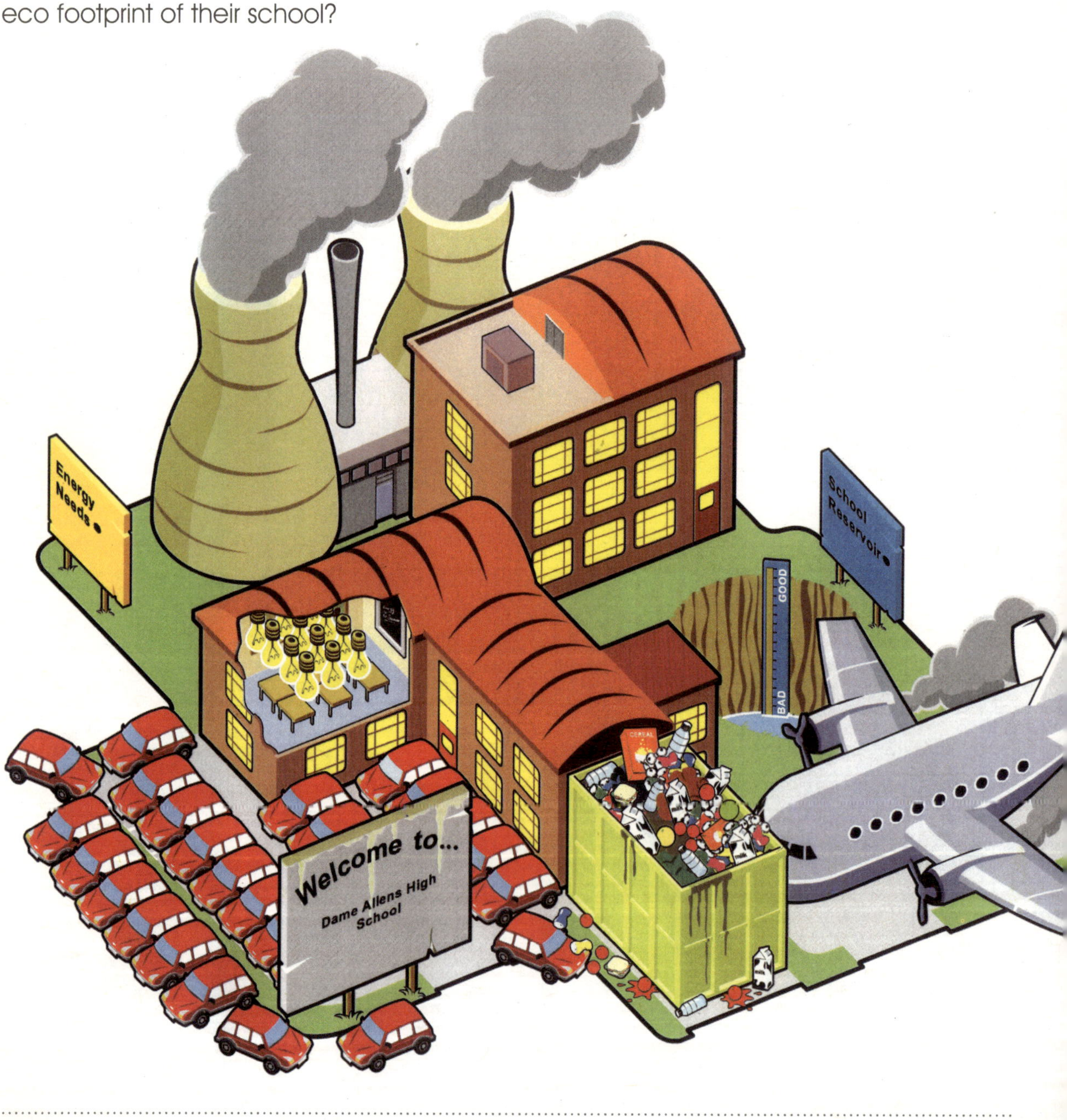

# Schools dispose of more than 60,000 tonnes of waste each year

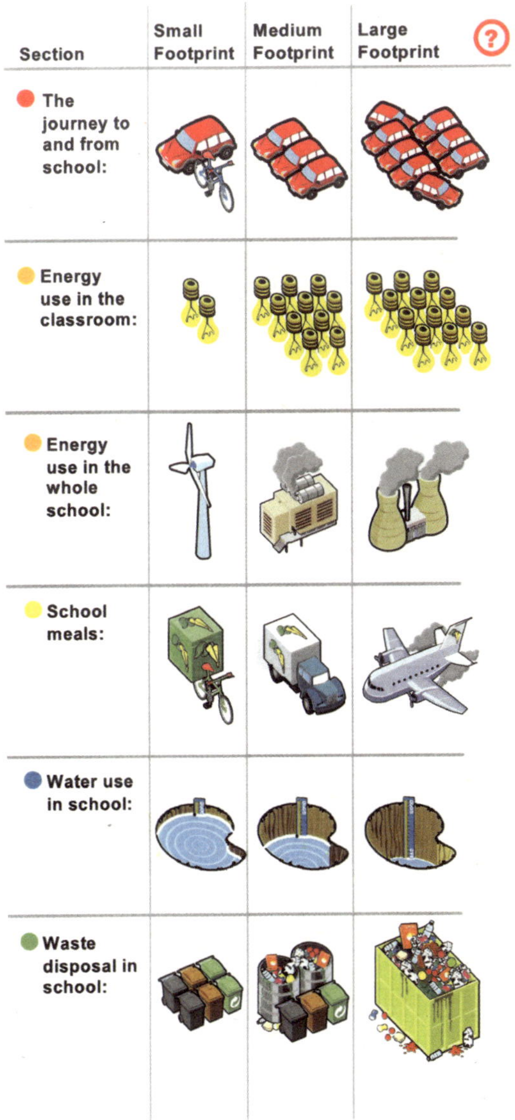


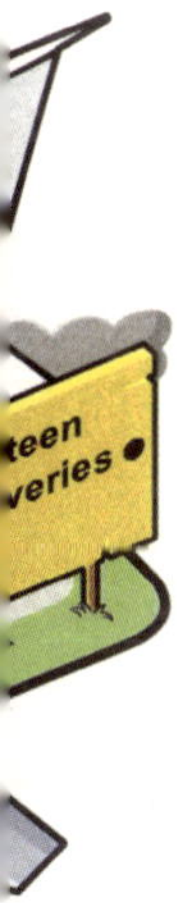

## The challenge of greener schools

Schools aren't the sorts of places you immediately equate with low-energy living. Many of them are old buildings with costly, outdated and inefficient heating and cooling systems that break down at the first hint of sun or snow. Others have poor levels of insulation, including creaky doors and draughty, ill-fitting windows.

And that's just the buildings. Vehicles taking students to and from school contribute a huge amount to the environmental damage caused by traffic. Food in schools is often wasteful, too: many schools spend a huge amount of money and energy preparing meals that few students really eat, the ingredients of which are grown and shipped in energy-intensive ways.

No wonder former education secretary Alan Johnson pledged a total of £110million over three years to make schools carbon neutral. But how can school students make a difference in this environment, and bring their imaginations to bear in a way that will be good for them and the environment? Dott 07's ECO Design Challenge aimed to find out.

Left: a graphic representation of energy usage by Dame Allen High School

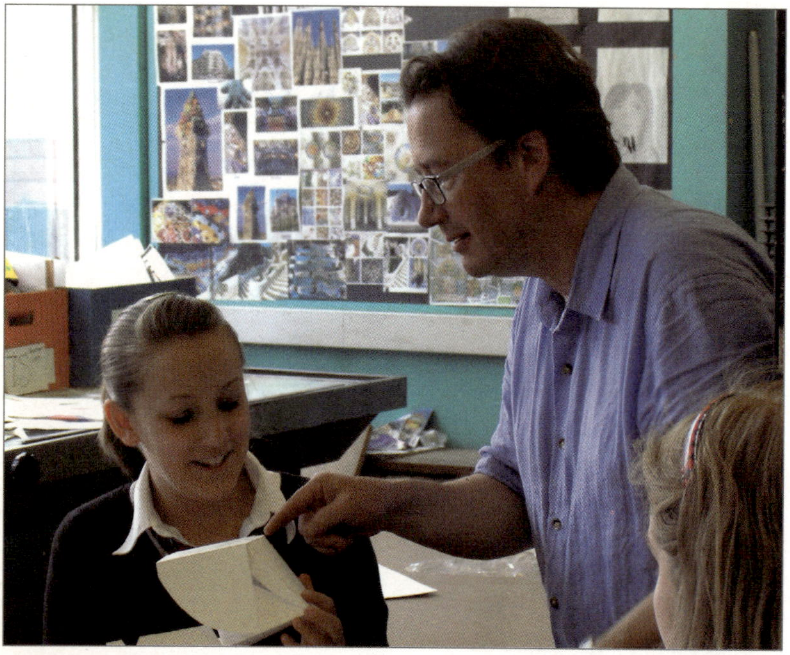

## How did the Eco Design Challenge work?

The project, which was designed to tie in with the UK National Curriculum, encouraged Year 8 students across the North East of England to channel their creativity into redesigning parts of their schools, with the objective of reducing their ecological and carbon footprints. It encouraged the design of new systems and products that support a sustainable future.

'The brief was to try to take design cross-curriculum in the context of sustainability,' says industrial designer Nick Devitt, Senior Producer on the project. 'We wanted to take design out of the technology workshop and give Year 8 students a broader "whole systems" perspective on how redesigning individual components could affect their school as a larger ecology.'

Dott posed two questions to a total of 80 schools: 'How big is your school's ecological footprint?' and 'What design actions do you propose to make it smaller?'

Their first step was to identify, using Dott's calculator, where the problems were in their school. Dott gave the schoolchildren a carbon ECO calculator Excel spreadsheet, as well as an animated Flash version of it, which allowed them to process their data and get a graphic illustration of their progress, like a school report.

They measured key resource flows, such as how much water is used, how waste is dealt with, how pupils actually get to school or where their food comes from. 'This measurement phase gave them a feel for how well their school was performing as a system,' explains Devitt.

They went on to use this data as a basis for a design brief that would lead to the feature in question working more effectively. Many of the students worked with professional designers to develop design responses to them. The results were showcased in a 'projects factory' at the Dott 07 Festival.

We learned that many children are already well informed about environmental issues. What Dott added was an opportunity to try out design techniques as a way to make a positive, practical difference.

To help the students, Dott invited professional designers and architects to spend time in some of the schools and work with the students. Both sides – the students and the designers – report that their enthusiasm was fired up and that their exchanges sped up the development of ideas.

**Above:** leading designer Sebastian Conran visited Lord Lawson of Beamish School to work with students on their projects

'The surprising thing was the amount of effort and gusto that the schools put into it,' says Devitt. Eighty-six schools registered to take part – nearly half of all schools in the region. Twenty of these were shortlisted and went on to work with the designers to develop ideas. The shortlisted 20 came up with a fascinating selection of design briefs, ranging from secret passages underground to pupils creating energy while in detention. There was also a heavy emphasis on issues of recycling.

One of the great side-effects of the challenge, according to Devitt, is that some of the students have gone out and talked to local businesses in a kind of reverse education process.

'They're little eco-police, little eco-warriors,' he says. 'You've got the adults who think they know it all and then 13-year-old enthusiastic people come along in a kind of reverse student placement. But they'll learn about how business works too.'

The best solutions were worked into a 'design factory', which formed a central part of the Dott 07 Festival.

A series of ECO Design Challenge Awards were also presented as part of the Creative Community Awards during the first week of the festival. But the real benefits of the project – for future school buildings, designers and the rest of us – could be a great deal bigger than any prize.

Below is a list of the five schools that were shortlisted for Creative Community Awards, which were awarded at the start of the Dott 07 Festival on Tuesday 16 October.

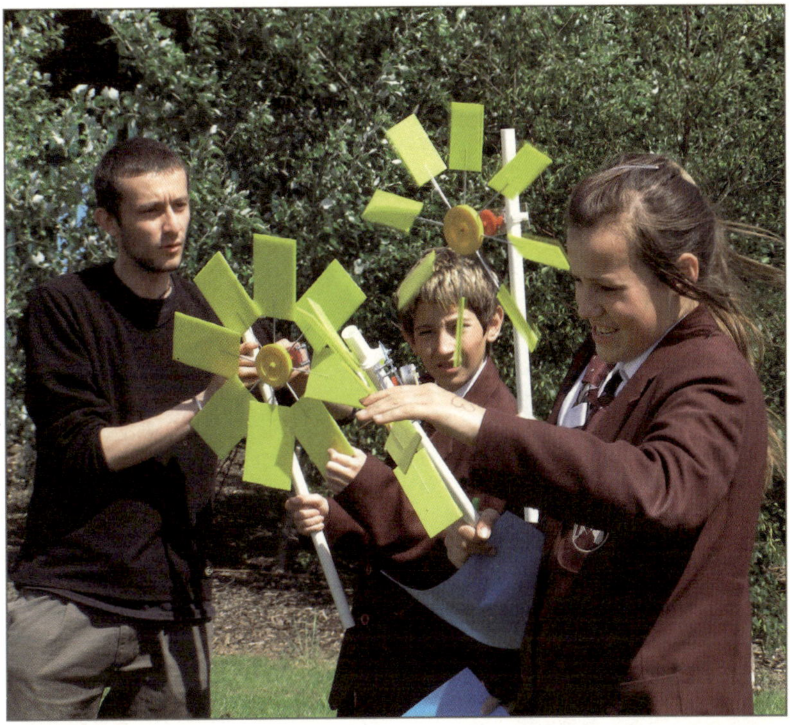

**Above:** Roy Shearer of Zero-waste Design works with students from MacMillan Academy

**Acklam Grange School, Middlesbrough**

The school's footprint highlighted a number of issues for the school to tackle. Students from Year 8 worked with three designers to develop their ideas, which included solar panels, filtration ponds and more. Their design for the ultimate school was shaped like a sun as a reminder of its design aims.

**Cleaswell Hill School, Choppington**

Food in our lunches can travel thousands of miles to our plates, so Cleaswell wanted to grow their own, which would also bring educational and energy benefits. A small team from Year 10 at Cleaswell, a school for students with learning difficulties, worked with their teacher Cathryn Hill on the project.

Stuart Franklin, an experienced architect with Jane Darbyshire and David Kendall Ltd, and recent design

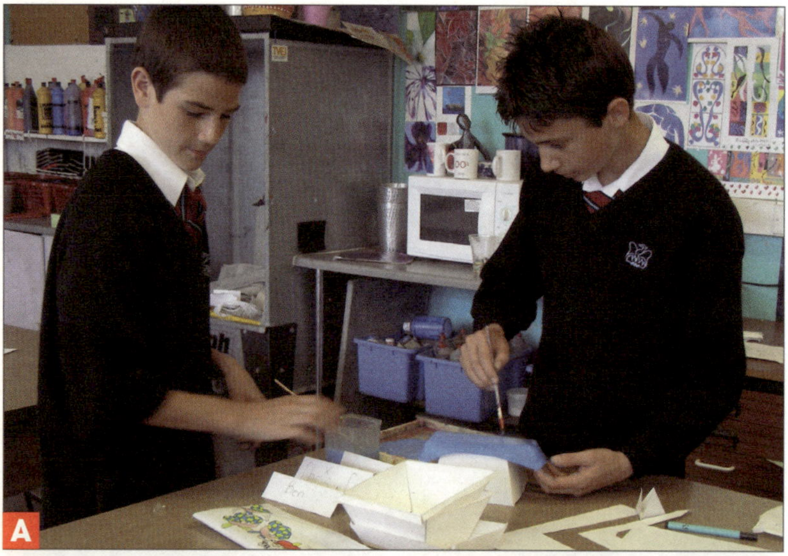

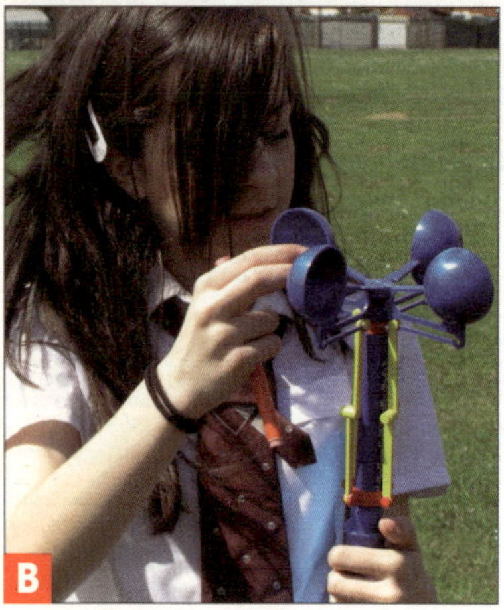

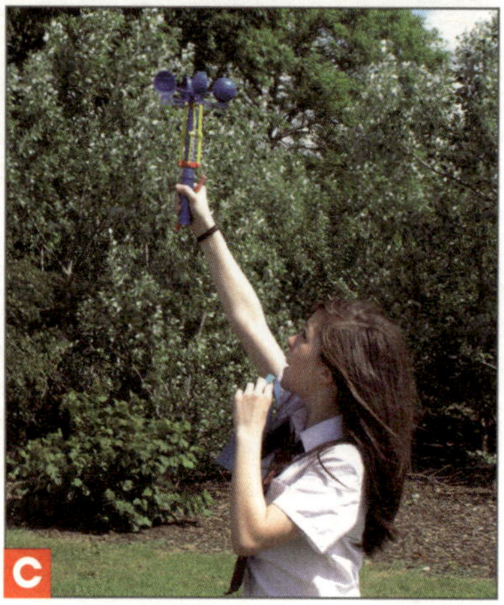

A: students at Lord Lawson of Beamish School get stuck in to their design projects
B&C: a student from MacMillan Academy takes part in the Eco Design Challenge

graduate Gillian Sanderson helped the school develop fun ideas for their Vegigrow garden. They designed a small garden with raised beds for easy access, conducted researched about what would grow and made plans for community involvement. Local allotment users have offered to assist the school with their gardens.

**Lord Lawson of Beamish School, Birtley**

The source of eco-concern for this team was how students and teachers travel to school. A group of 40 Geography students calculated the school's carbon footprint, and then Denise Taylor's Design and Technology class worked on design ideas. Michael Atkinson, an architect from Newcastle firm Purves Ash LLP, helped the group to develop their transport ideas. With a brand new school building on the way, the students designed a new system of bike sheds to encourage students to cycle to school, which they hope will be implemented for the new school.

**St Hild's Church of England School, Hartlepool**

This team concentrated on how to reduce the water wastage in their school. Twenty-three Year 8 students determined the school's carbon footprint and another 24 developed ideas with teachers Diane Crannage and Mike Rowe.

Alex Reeves, an architecture student from Newcastle University, visited the school to provide additional advice. Their solution was a curved, transparent extension on to the school's roofs to collect rainwater, channelling it onto a water wheel to generate electricity and then on into storage tanks. The extension would enable everyone to see just how much water and energy was being saved.

**Tanfield School, Stanley**

The students at Tanfield wanted a place where both they and the local community could learn about the environment and growing and cooking food, but that would also help to reduce the school's carbon and ecological footprint.

Fourteen students worked with Dr Kev Hilton, a designer from the Centre for Design Research at Northumbria University, and with teachers Stephen Mason and Sue Smith to develop their design.

The Tanfield Bubble is an outdoor, glass-enclosed eco-classroom designed to provide education on sustainable development, and has already received a good deal of local support. The Bubble would include areas to grow fruit and vegetables, kitchen classrooms in which to cook them and a café in which to sell them, as well as chickens, beehives, rainwater collection – and even a wormery.

## What next?

Dott's Eco Design Challenge unleashed extraordinary energy and creativity in schools across the region. Students embraced a new vision of education in which people of all ages assume responsibility for creating and enjoying a sustainable future.

As we go to press with this manual, the National Endowment for Science Technology and the Arts (NESTA) and the Design Council are finalising details of an Eco Design Challenge Phase 2 for the five finalists of this year's challenge. Email Lesley Morris at the Design Council: lesley.morris@designcouncil.org.uk

**Carbon Detectives Kit**

At a national level the Department for Children, Schools and Families (DCSF) has teamed up with the World Wildlife Fund to launch a Carbon Detectives Kit. 37,000 UK schools may compare results.
www.carbondetectives.org.uk

**NESTA**

www.nesta.org.uk/news

**Education for Sustainable Development**

The United Nations University is setting up a worldwide system centres which will gather together local networks of educational organisations and establishments. The North East's coordinator is the Institute for Research on Environment and Sustainability (IRES) at Newcastle University.
www.ncl.ac.uk/environment/research/EfSDVision.htm
or email Dr Aidan Doyle: Aidan.Doyle@ncl.ac.uk

**Carbon Control**

The RSA has teamed up with Tesco to distribute its Schools Carbon Calculator. The project will culminate in a nationwide three week competition.
www.rsacarbonlimited.org

**One World Schools**

Groundwork helps schools move from bronze and silver EcoSchools awards through to Green Flag status.
http://penninelancs.groundworknw.org.uk

**Sustainable School Self-Evaluation Kit**

www.teachernet.gov.uk/sustainableschools/tools

The team behind the project is listed on pages 96 to 99. For other information on Eco Design Challenge go to the Dott website:
www.dott07.com/go/ecodesignchallenge

# OurNewSchool: how could schools be better designed?

**Wouldn't it be great if...** the whole community decided how its new school would be designed?

## The future of school design

Having proclaimed the vital importance of education to the nation's future, the government is putting its money where its mouth is. Over the next 15 years, 3,500 schools will be rebuilt or refurbished in a £70billion programme called Building Schools for the Future (BSF). It is a fantastic opportunity to put the latest thinking on education into practice on a massive scale.

A lot of attention is being paid to the criteria that will determine how all these schools will be designed. Head teachers and communities, and the architects and designers they work with, will be nominally free to do things their way. But their design space will be heavily circumscribed by public procurement procedures that determine how all this public money may be spent. If they were left unchanged, procurement policies would force local authorities to go with the lowest-cost proposals for slightly better versions of the types of school that were there before.

There are positive signs that a broader definition of value for money, which concentrates on more than just cost, will inform the BSF process.

Powerful government agencies including the Audit Commission have stated that outputs – such as the impact of new school projects on the local economy – are as important as inputs, such as the money spent on them.

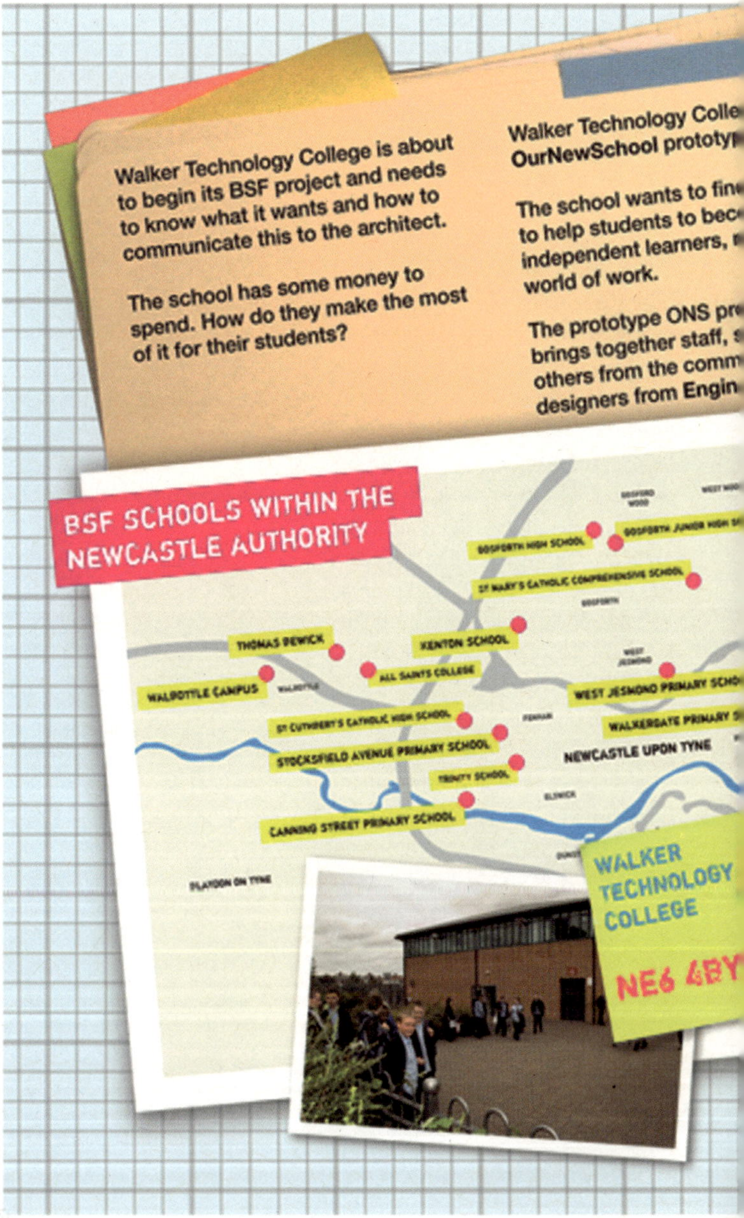


PHOTOS: Phyllis Christoper GRAPHIC: Engine

**What we did:** the OurNewSchool project brought together information and views from everyone involved in the life of Walker Technology College

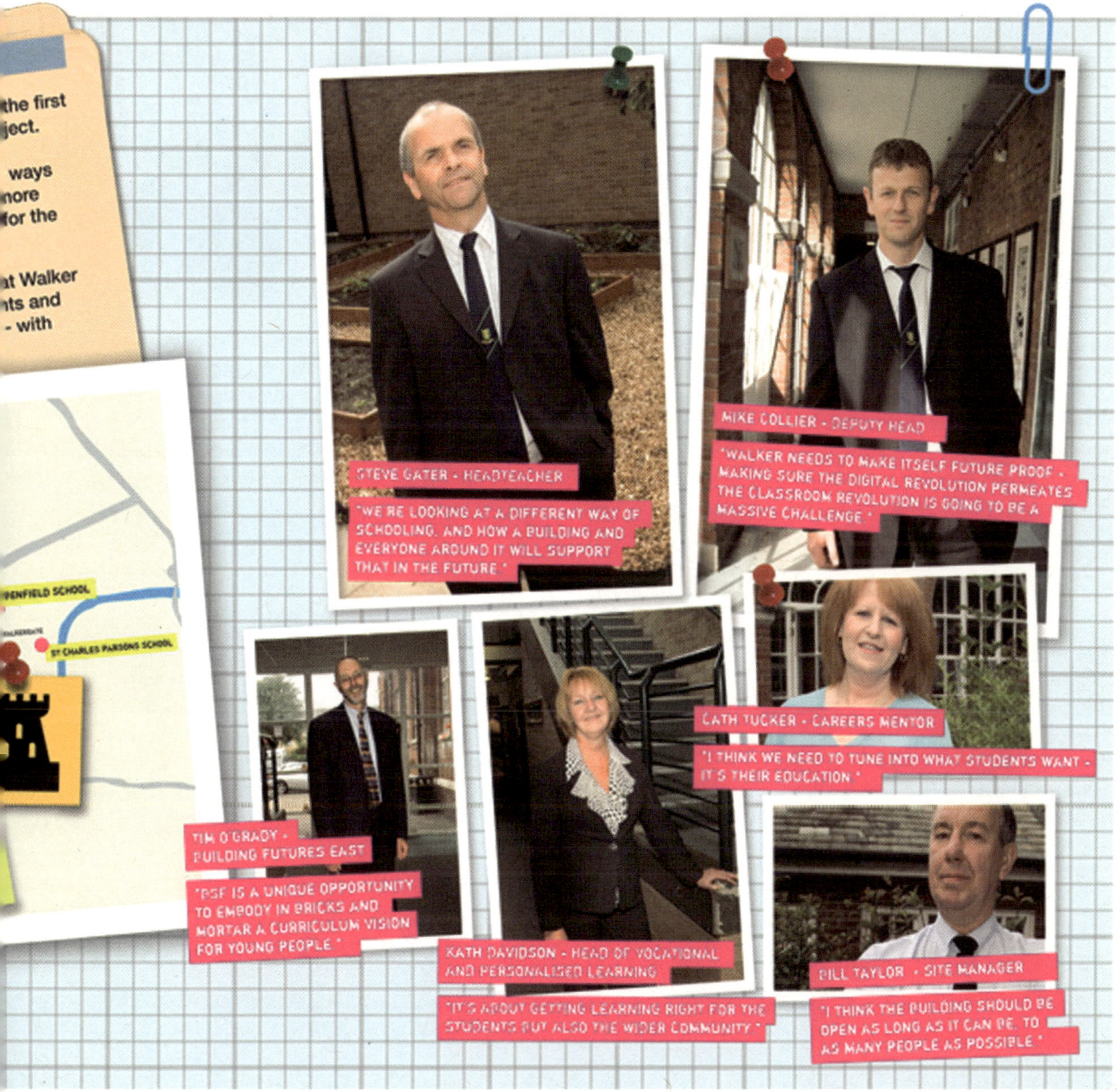

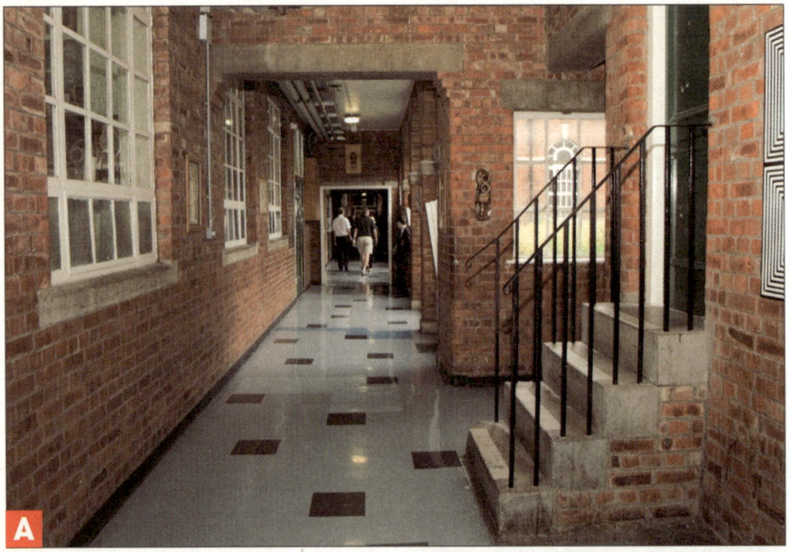

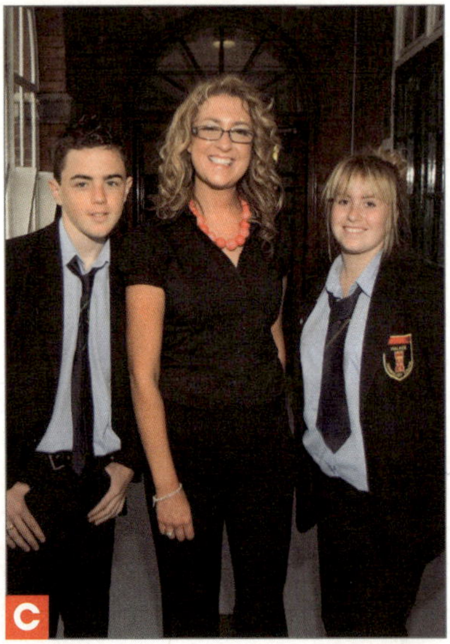

## How OurNewSchool worked

What are the design priorities when a school is rebuilt? This was the question posed by designers from co-design team Engine, led by Joe Heapy, when they created an in-school design laboratory at Walker Technology College in Newcastle, one of the first schools in England to receive money from the government's BSF project. Their aim was to enable all members of the community to explore options for the school's development and they learned a great deal about how a school can make itself 'design ready'. The team began by embarking on a discovery phase, working with pupils and finding out everything about their experiences of the school day. They went on to hold workshops on the subject of time and how the school

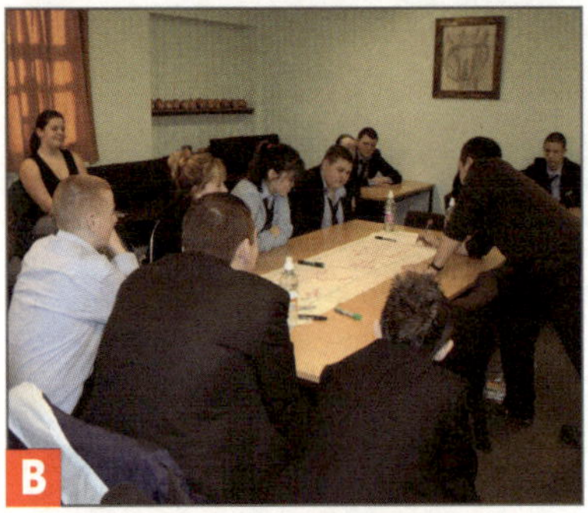

A: inside Walker Technology College
B: Joe Heapy from Engine works with students and teachers at Walker
C: student council members James Oliphant and Amber Milligen with Walker teacher Claire Goodwill. Claire recently retrained to teach hair and beauty at Walker's vocational block

might use it better. Engine worked with the teachers and students to identify a series of issues that needed addressing. One example was: 'If we waste time at the beginning of a lesson because not all pupils have pens, then a system is needed that ensures every pupil has a pen'. The main topic to emerge from their discussions was vocational learning. It was agreed that the benefits to the school in having their own co-designed vocational learning zone would be numerous. For example, it would reduce time wasted travelling to outside vocational learning facilities and provide more choice and better opportunities for pupils. Engine and the students considered how this vocational learning zone might be best provided for Year 7 up to Year 14 in a way that would be sustainable, adaptable, and could potentially serve the wider community. They then organised small workshops with the BSF team, Walker head teacher Steve Gater, deputy head Mike Collier and Kath Davidson, head of personalised learning.

PHOTOS: A, C & E – Phyllis Christoper; B & D – Engine

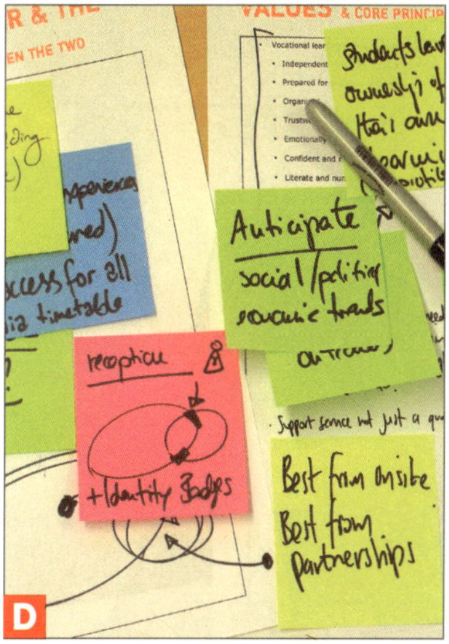


D

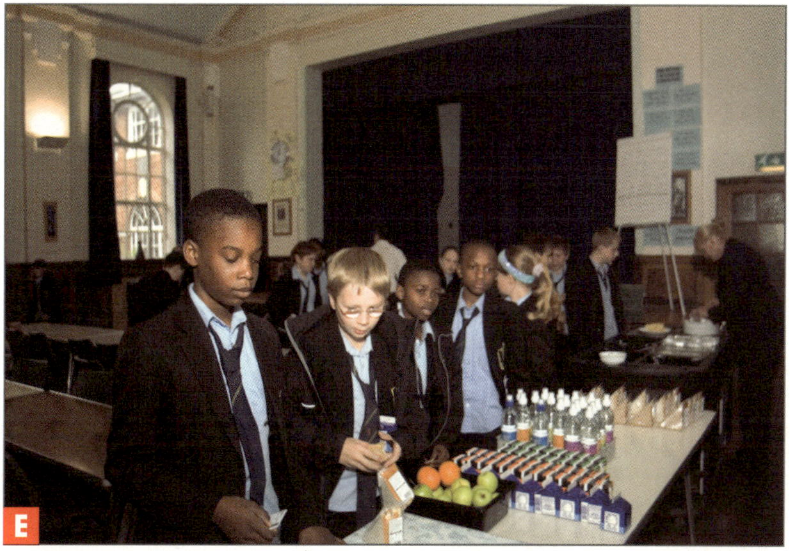

E

## New ways to learn

Nearly 40 years ago, Ivan Illich proposed that we should de-school society[14]. His idea was that we should use existing technologies and spaces – the telephone, local radio, town hall meetings – to create learning webs through which learners could connect with their peers and with new contexts in which to learn.

Three decades later, Tom Bentley of Demos made a similar point in *Learning Beyond the Classroom*[15]: 'We should think of learning as an ecology of people and groups, projects, tools and infrastructures. We need to reconceptualise education as a living system whose intelligence is distributed and shared among all its participants.'

## What next?

Details are still being looked at for the proposed vocational learning block and the design of the learning journey for students through school. The team is considering questions such as: what subjects will Walker keep on site? Who will use the vocational learning block? How will the block help to build links with local employers? How will it serve the wider community?

Engine is putting together a design brief in the form of a brochure that will be used by the school to help them present designs developed through the project. The brochure will include drawings, photographs and illustrated scenarios to bring the school's ideas to life for parents, partners and the Local Education Partnership, the organisation that will be working with them to develop their new school.

The OurNewSchool project at Walker Technology College is a prototype for a way of working that aims to support schools in designing together. The plan is to see if the prototype can be transformed into a larger project, creating a design community of schools and developing new skills.

If you'd like to know more or would like to help, go to:
www.ournewschool.org or
www.enginegroup.co.uk

The team behind OurNewSchool is listed on pages 96 to 99.

For more information go to:
www.dott07.com/go/ournewschool

**D:** Engine worked with students and teachers to find out everything about their school day
**E:** lunchtime at Walker

# Health: can design make a difference?

One planet living is not just about looking after the natural world. It also means improving the ways we organise social support for each other on issues such as health.

Health and care industries are growing because people don't look after family members as much as they once did. The world's poorest nations spend 200 times less money per person on health (an average of $11) than wealthier nations such as Britain or the US, which averages $5,000 a head[16].

The pity of it is that spending larger sums of money does not appear to buy better health – or, at least, not a longer life. The biggest spenders on healthcare, North Americans, die earlier than Japanese or Spaniards, who spend far less[17]. Medicine is now a $2trillion industry but much of the world's population dies of the same diseases that killed people 1,000 years ago: malaria, tuberculosis and malnutrition.

## Counting the uncountable

Our starting point in Dott was that care is a time and communication issue, not a technology or drugs issue. The costs of technology (including drugs and hospitals) can be counted, and are. The value of health professionals, and the time spent by people being off work ill, also has a financial cost. But the time spent by caregivers looking after loved ones tends not to be counted, let alone acknowledged, as an economic activity plus in the nation's balance sheet.

It makes no sense to ignore this care economy. Study after study tells us that a sense of social support is a buffer against stress and illness. A strong support system lowers the likelihood of many illnesses, decreases the length of recovery time, and reduces the probability of mortality from serious diseases.

Wireless first-aid alarms and distress-call systems are useful and reassuring. But, by far the most beneficial care for people of all ages, not just elders, is social contact and mutual support.

# Alzheimer100: Better Lives With Dementia

**Wouldn't it be great if…** practical steps were taken to improve daily life for people with dementia and their carers?

**Informal caregivers – family, friends and neighbours – spend 80 hours a week providing care[18]**

**Dementia already affects 750,000 people in the UK. The number will be approaching two million by 2050, with three or four times as many people affected indirectly[19]**

## How Alzheimer100 worked

Dott 07 asked service design firm thinkpublic, led by Deborah Szebeko, to work with Alzheimer's Society branches throughout the North East to investigate the everyday problems experienced by Alzheimer's patients and carers, and service providers. thinkpublic helped people record their experiences; they used film, diaries, interviewed one another, made prototypes, and drew. From these activities emerged a long list of common challenges faced by people during their journeys through dementia.

**The key challenges identified were:**

- Social isolation, both of people with dementia and their carers
- Lack of public awareness and the stigma attached to the subject
- Difficulty in navigating the wide array of support services that exist
- Tendency of carers and services to be over-protective of people with dementia
- The long hours worked by carers on their own and without support.

## Case study 1 – Bill

Bill, 56, was an engineer for the whole of his working life. He lives with his wife, Susan, in the city. His two children live a 15-minute drive away.

His story: 'My life's changed a lot over the past couple of years. Being diagnosed with Alzheimer's means I have to rely on my family much more. I'm lucky that I have a good group of friends – at first it was a bit strange, but they're beginning to understand that I'm still me.

'One of the hardest things for me was losing my job. Things that I was doing every day I just couldn't remember. This meant we lost an income and went on disability allowance, but what amazed me most was how much I missed my workmates.

'I've more time to enjoy my hobbies, and I've also been introduced to other groups in similar situations to me by my GP. The fun and humour of the group get me through the tough days.

'I couldn't have got through this without Susan. Sometimes we argue and get frustrated, but we both support each other and that gets us through.'

## Case study 2 – Betty

Betty is 80 and lives alone – her children live a long way away. She is a retired schoolteacher and her husband Alan passed away 10 years ago. Betty was diagnosed with Alzheimer's two years later and is now in the later stages of the disease.

Her story: 'I felt very isolated when I was diagnosed with Alzheimer's. My family wasn't around me and I wasn't referred for support by the doctor. For a few years I felt very lonely – I had nothing to do and no one to see. All I thought about was the past, which made me feel content. I started to look for my old home and my neighbour says I spent hours searching.

'I now attend a day club where I have lunch and have made new friends. I always feel safe there, even though I can't remember everyone's name. It's good to talk to people: I talk about my life, my family, where I was brought up. My neighbour says that I don't wander as much any more.'

## Case study 3 – Margaret

Before Margaret, now 72, married her husband Howard, she worked at her village bank. She then had three children and gave up work to look after them and the family home. Margaret's children have since grown up and left the area and she has been diagnosed with vascular dementia.

Her story: 'I went to see a consultant who diagnosed that I had a "memory problem". A memory problem? Everybody my age starts to have a bad memory!

'Howard keeps saying that I'm forgetting things, but I don't know what the fuss is about. He says that

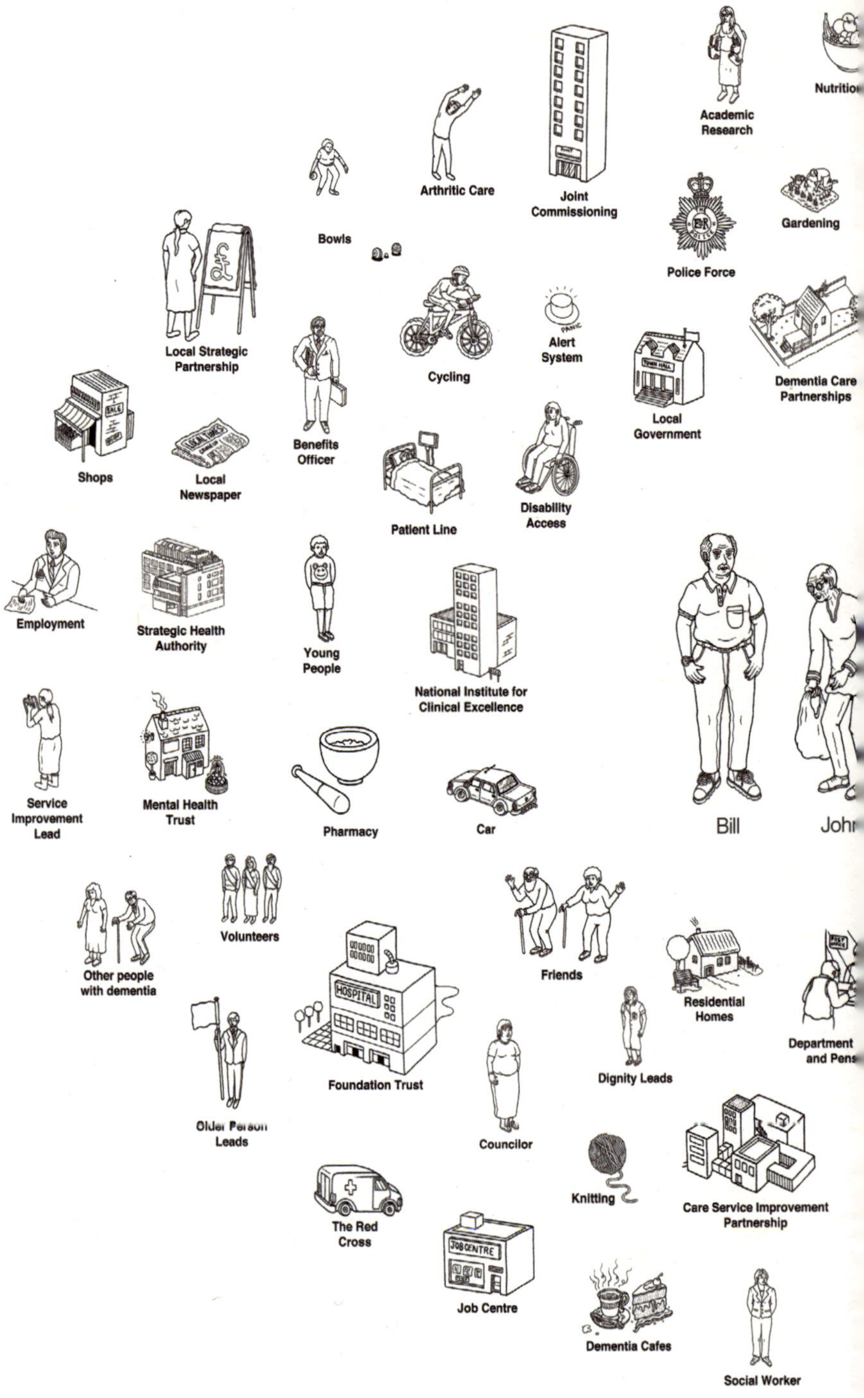

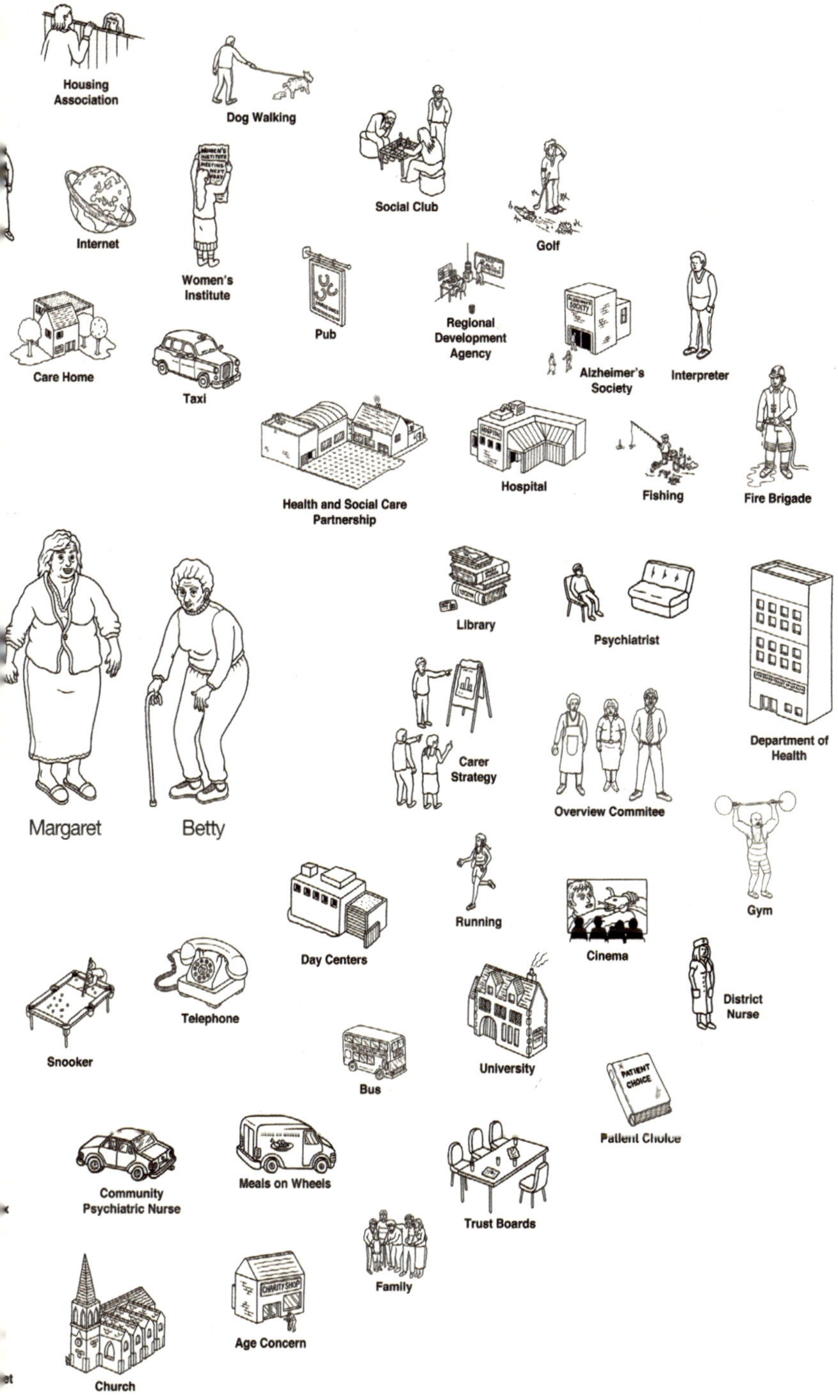


we need to tell the children, but what's to tell them? We can look after ourselves.

'I used to host afternoon tea for the Women's Institute every week, but I'm too busy at the moment. Howard says that I should be seeing people more – he keeps talking about a day club that I should go to. Day club? I'm not old enough for that yet!'

## Case study 4 – Johnny

Johnny is a 73-year-old former sailor whose one son who lives abroad. Shortly after Johnny was diagnosed with dementia, his wife Mary died.

His story: 'I miss Mary so much. I didn't realise how much I relied on her. I'm so confused now. I can't even remember when I have a doctor's appointment, let alone get there.

'Luckily, I now have someone to remind me about appointments and a volunteer who accompanies me. They also attach notes to household objects to remind me about engagements and to prompt me to take my medication.

'I have also been introduced to a volunteer service that sends people to visit and check that I am well.'

**Left:** when someone first discovers that they or a loved one may have a problem with dementia, a key challenge is the complexity of support services and information available. Citizens and professionals jointly considered this challenge in a co-design workshop during Alzheimer100. Their conclusion: it would be great if there was a Dementia Adviser in each area, supported by a kind of concierge service in the background to guide people through the early stages.

ILLUSTRATION: thinkpublic/Matt Johnstone

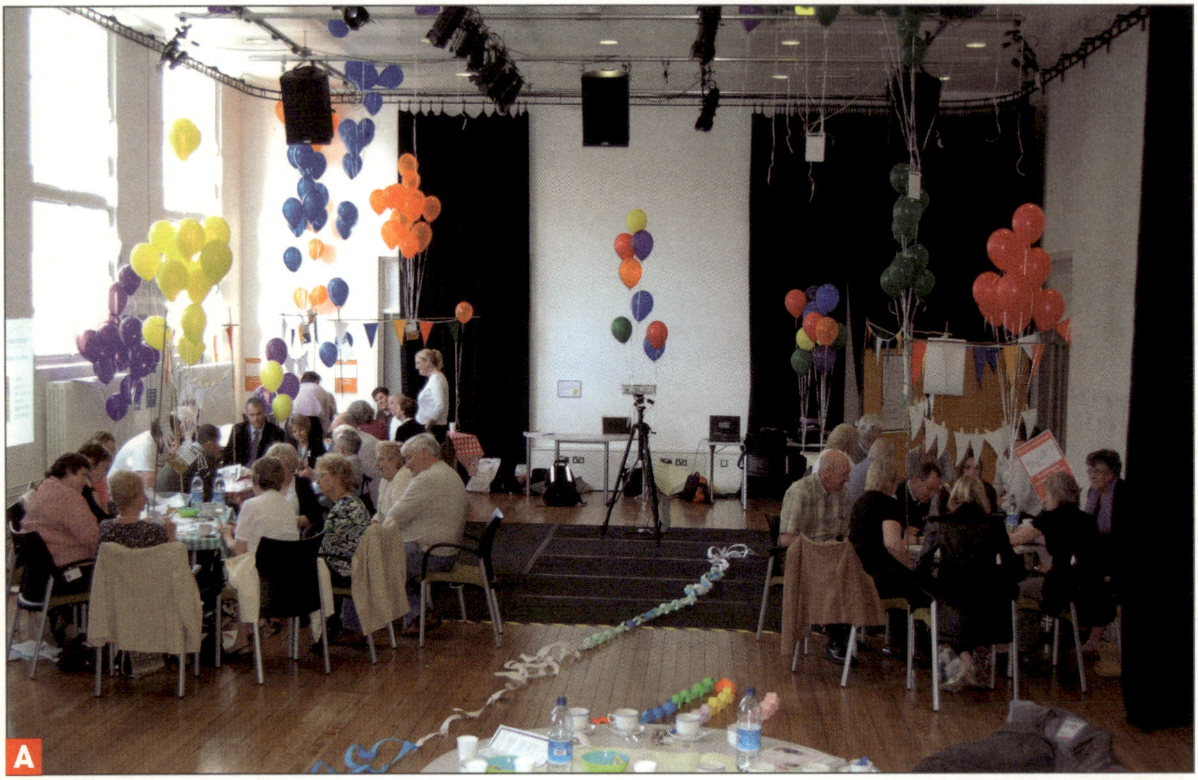

A: Dott hosted several co-design days at which people listened to each other's stories and voted (in this case using balloons) on which challenges were most important to them
B: one of the creative workshops organised by Equal Arts

## Proposal 1: Dementia Adviser Concierge Service

One of the key challenges faced by people when they first discover they or a loved one may have dementia is the sheer complexity of support services and information available. A co-design workshop led by thinkpublic concluded that it would be advantageous if there was a key person to help guide people through the early stages of dementia.

## Proposal 2: TimeBank for volunteers

One way to reduce individual caregiver stress is to spread care between more than one person. One theme to emerge from Alzheimer100 was that friends and family often want to help but don't know how. With 'time banks', mutual volunteers help each other to remain independent. Volunteers earn and pay 'time credits' through the scheme for giving and receiving non-medical services such as shopping, friendly visits, bill-paying, hospital visits, home repairs, walking clubs, support groups and self-help courses. For the Dott 07 Festival, Dott teamed up with TimeBank to demonstrate how a service for a different group of people works – in this case, refugees and their mentors. The service, called Time Together (www.timetogether.org.uk) featured mentors and mentees from the North of England Refugee Service in Newcastle and Sunderland.

Time Together works as a three-tier system whose staff use the 'Time Together Tool Kit'. As a poster at the Dott 07 Festival boldly asked: 'Wouldn't it be great if we had a

PHOTOS: Thinkpublic, Equal Arts

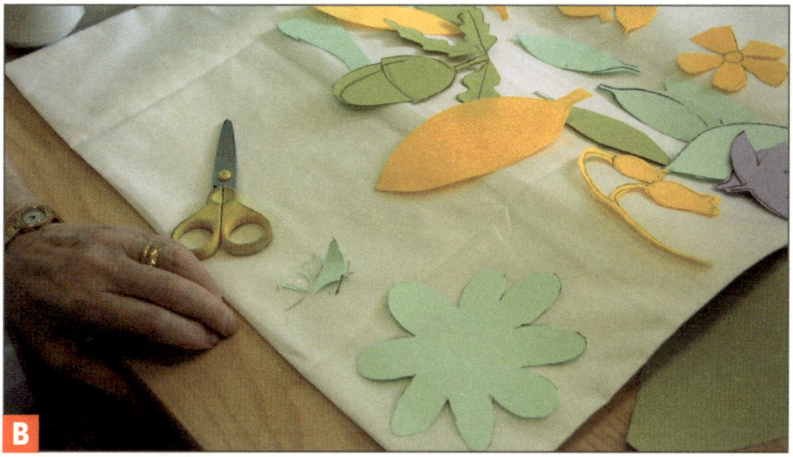

Time Together for carers?' Volunteer researchers from the Alzheimer's Society solicited feedback from visitors on how such a service should work if one were set up for volunteers to share some of the load of carers of people with dementia.

## Proposal 3: Dementia Café

Another co-design workshop discussed the stigma attached to the subject of dementia, and how difficult it is for people with dementia or their carers to talk openly about the subject. Dementia needs to be spoken about openly in the community, and people with dementia need to be able to meet other people in a social space where they can talk and have fun. It turned out that the prototype of an answer to this need already exists in the form of the Dementia Café set up and run by volunteers in North East England.

## Proposal 4: Wandering Path (Equal Arts, Shadon House)

Steel picket fencing and grey concrete are bad for morale and do little to stimulate the imagination. And yet many of the institutions for carers or people with dementia are just this depressing. Equal Arts, a foundation that enables older people to be involved in arts across the North East, plans to create a series of 'wandering paths' through the grounds of Shadon House, a dementia resource centre in Gateshead. Safe wandering can be of huge benefit to people with dementia – but too often, they encounter locked doors or are told to sit down. Artists and horticulturists are beginning to develop plans with the involvement of older residents, care staff, families and the wider community.

## What next?

The Dott 07 team was inspired during the Alzheimer100 project by how much people with dementia, and their carers, do to support each other. That said, the project revealed new opportunities to improve peoples' lives in practical ways. Our project partners (below) will develop these ideas, presented at the Dott 07 festival, in the coming months.

**Alzheimer's Society**
The UK's leading care and research charity for people with dementia, their families and carers.
www.alzheimers.org.uk

**Years Ahead**
The North East regional forum on ageing.
www.yearsahead.org.uk

**Time Bank**
A national charity that inspires and connects people to volunteer in their communities.
www.timebank.org.uk

**thinkpublic**
London-based design firm specialising in user-focused design.
http://thinkpublic.com/

**Dementia Cafe**
A site where those involved with dementia can share experiences.
www.dementiacafe.com/news.php

**Equal Arts**
information@equalarts.org.uk
www.equalarts.org.uk

For further information on Alzheimer100 see:
www.dott07.com/go/alzheimer100

# DaSH: how can sexual health services be made easier to access?

**Wouldn't it be great if...** people who needed to use sexual health services did?

The UK has worryingly high rates of sexually transmitted infections (STIs) and the highest teenage pregnancy rate in Europe, and the North East commonly tops national figures. While Gateshead has had considerable success in bringing down teenage pregnancy rates – 22% in the past five years[20], due largely to taking the services out of their conventional settings and encouraging more young men to use them – local people still have to travel out of the town to get tested for STIs. The government has therefore given the health services money to create a local service.

**Britain has the dubious honour of coming second highest in the developed world league table for rates of teenage pregnancy[21]**

## How did DaSH work?

DaSH was a collaboration between Dott 07 and Gateshead Primary Care Trust (PCT), who worked together on design actions that would make sexual health screening and treatment services easier to access and use. The project aimed to develop a system where people would be seen by a local service within 48 hours of contact, and where the treatment path is clearly explained and suits the user's needs.

The team, led by Dr Louise Hulton of Design Options, began by conducting research to understand the daily lives of the people that policy-makers hope will use the service. They then explored ways that new facilities, communications and procedures could improve the use and experience of the service. Their final task was to deliver a service design blueprint covering these hard and soft issues to the district's PCT.

This project was carried out by Design Options, part of the technical assistance arm of Marie Stopes International, working together with Gateshead's Sexual Health Promotions team, with support from the Centre for Design Research at Northumbria University.

The Department for Health's National Strategy for Sexual Health and HIV suggests that users find that the services offering contraception and the diagnosis and treatment are disjointed, and they are in locations which are difficult to use or make the user feel stigmatised.

Sexual health workers in Gateshead already take their contraception services out to the user – for example, workers will meet young men and women at places where they usually gather, at school, leisure centres or in their homes.

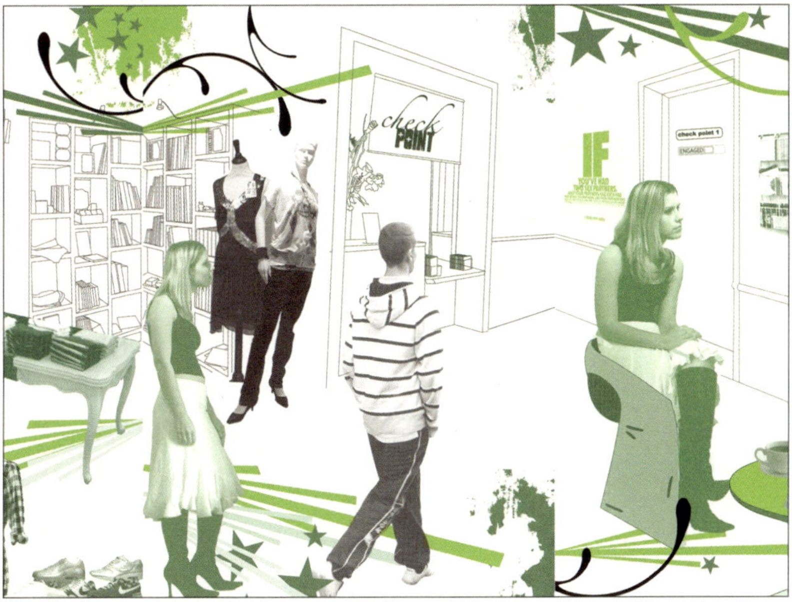


**Above: wouldn't it be great if sexual health clinics were placed in everyday situations? Clinic areas at the back of high street fashion stores, for example, might encourage people to look after their sexual health as part of their normal lifestyle**

But once screening or treatment for a sexually transmitted infection is needed, Newcastle or South Shields are currently the nearest places where facilities are available. This is often a long way to travel for those without personal transport, limited time or income, so it's easy for people to fall through the net.

The team's objective was to create a local service better suiting Gateshead residents so they are treated easier and quicker. The benefits of early diagnosis and treatment obviously include better health for the user, as well as a decreased risk of sexually transmitted infections being spread.

To design this service, the Design Options team spoke to around 40 professionals and more than 1,000 Gateshead citizens, with a particular focus on young people, gay and bisexual men, and other groups who find it harder to use health services. Interviews and discussions took place to ensure the final outcome met with their expectations and preferences. Each group looked at the ideas that the design team developed and explained what they would want their experience of the service to be like.

Taking the information gathered at these sessions, the designers looked at how their ideas would work in reality by working alongside the people who would be putting them into practice.

This is the first time sexual health service design has been tackled in this way and it's hoped the project will provide a good example of how to redevelop and advance other health services, both nationally and internationally. Unfriendly-by-design sexual health clinics can be unwelcoming, deterring those who really need them.

## What next?

DaSH, led by Design Options together with Gateshead PCT and the Centre for Design Research, Northumbria University, used the latest service design techniques to develop a sexual health service blueprint for the town. The project's founding principle was that a person's experience of using such a service should be central to its design.

The project team's design recommendations resulted in a blueprint for a service in which people are seen within 48 hours of first contact, the treatment pathway is clear and it meets the needs, preferences and circumstances of all users.

A reorganisation of the local health authorities means that implementing the DaSH-designed service is still in the pipeline, but the blueprints can be downloaded from: www.dott07.com/go dashconclusion

This user-centred approach for developing sexual health services has been picked up by five other health authorities, so the project's legacy continues. For more information, visit: www.designoptions.org.uk

The project team is listed on pages 96 to 99. For more about DaSH, visit: www.dott07.com/go/dash

ILLUSTRATION: Design Options with Louise Marshall (illustrator)

**Right:** designing a user-centred health service, as DaSH set out to do, is not a simple matter. As this chart shows, DaSH involved contact between an extraordinary variety of people, groups and organisations. The designers in DaSH spent a huge amount of time making initial contact with people and gaining their trust, before they even started on co-design activities

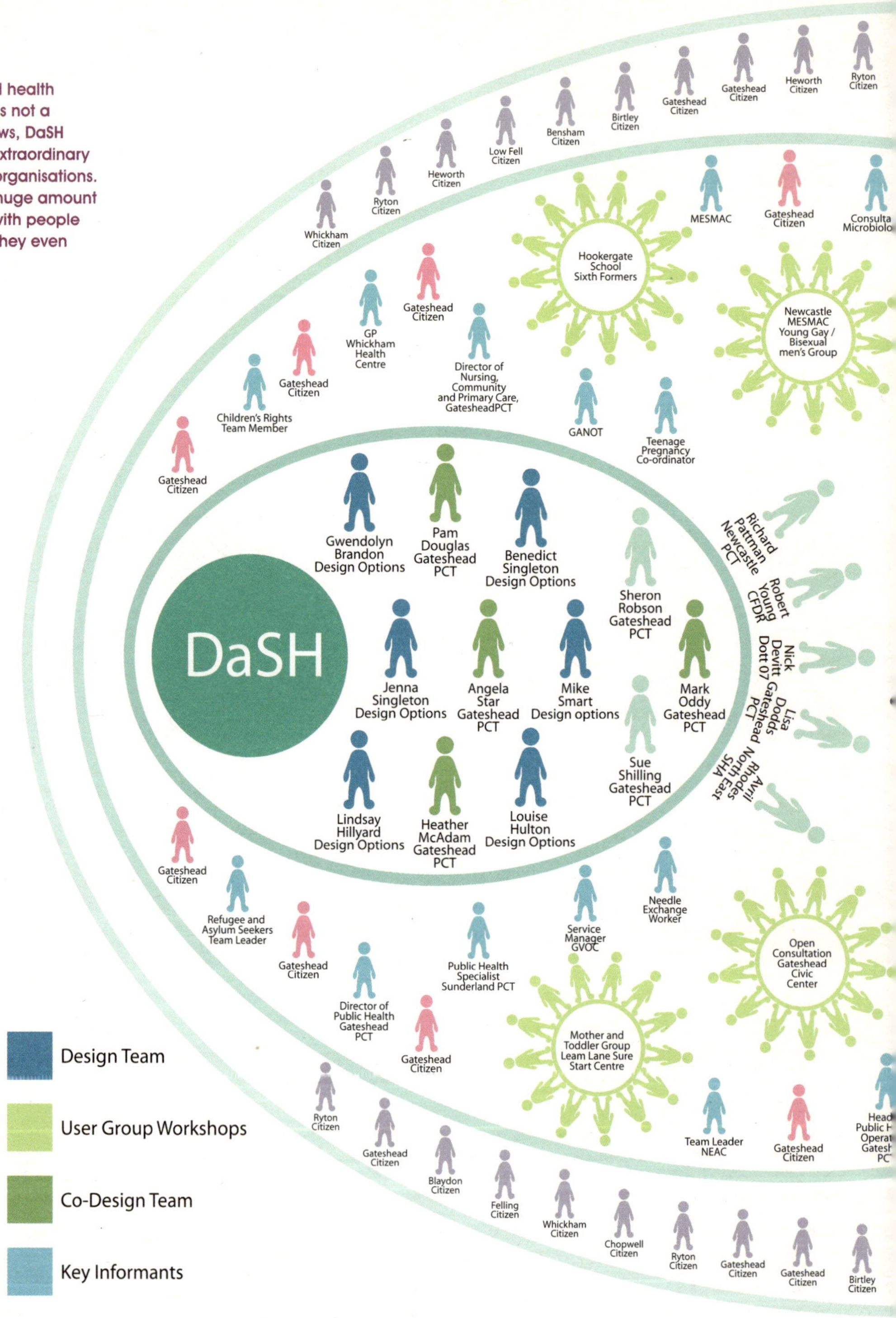


ILLUSTRATION: Design Options

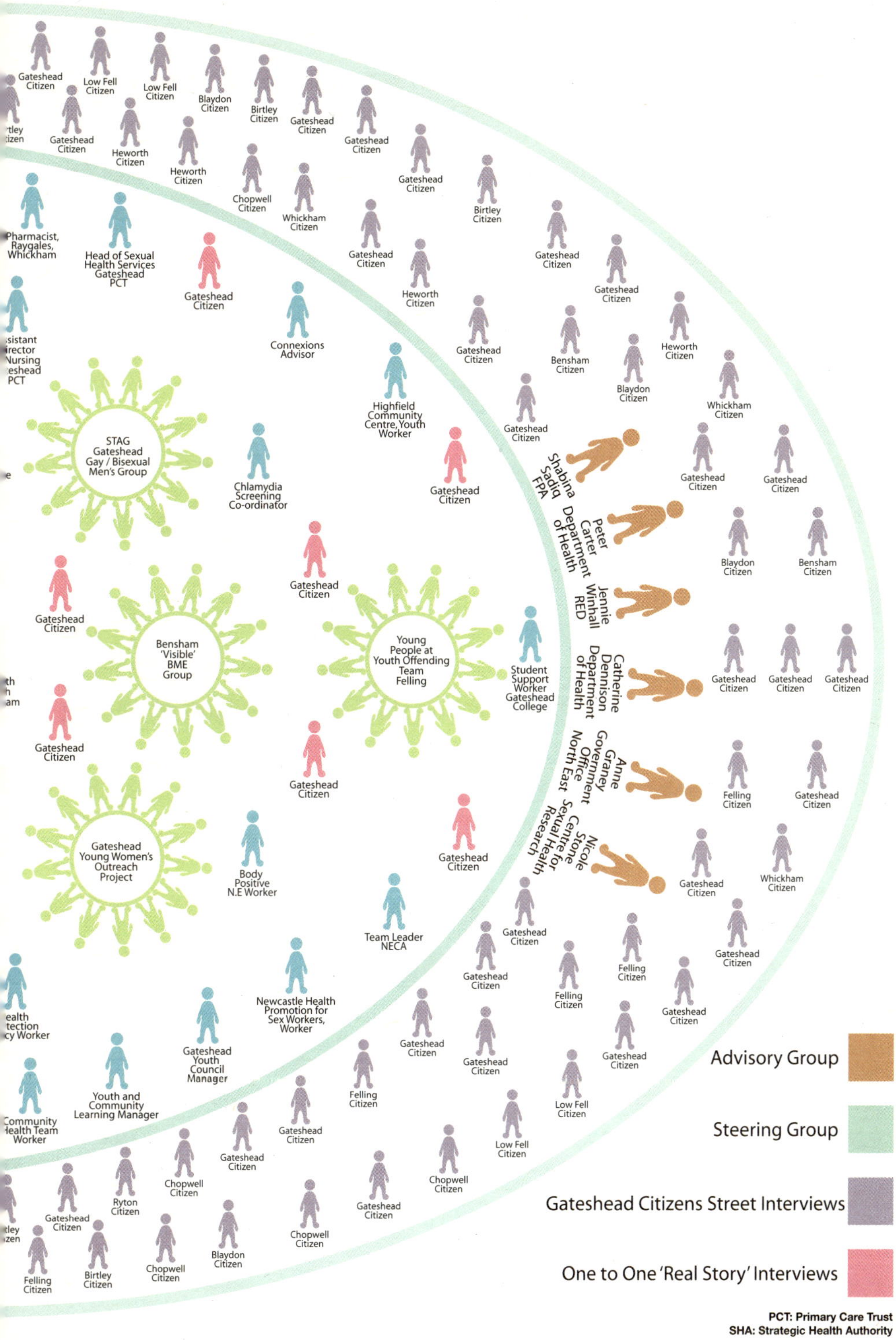
Gateshead Citizen
Low Fell Citizen
Low Fell Citizen
Blaydon Citizen
Birtley Citizen
Gateshead Citizen
Gateshead Citizen
Gateshead Citizen
Heworth Citizen
Heworth Citizen
Chopwell Citizen
Whickham Citizen
Gateshead Citizen
Birtley Citizen
Gateshead Citizen
Heworth Citizen
Gateshead Citizen
Gateshead Citizen
Gateshead Citizen
Bensham Citizen
Blaydon Citizen
Heworth Citizen
Whickham Citizen
Gateshead Citizen
Gateshead Citizen
Gateshead Citizen
Blaydon Citizen
Bensham Citizen
Gateshead Citizen
Gateshead Citizen
Gateshead Citizen
Felling Citizen
Gateshead Citizen
Gateshead Citizen
Whickham Citizen
Gateshead Citizen
Gateshead Citizen
Felling Citizen
Gateshead Citizen
Felling Citizen
Gateshead Citizen
Gateshead Citizen
Gateshead Citizen
Gateshead Citizen
Felling Citizen
Low Fell Citizen
Low Fell Citizen
Gateshead Citizen
Chopwell Citizen
Gateshead Citizen
Chopwell Citizen
Gateshead Citizen
Chopwell Citizen
Ryton Citizen
Gateshead Citizen
Blaydon Citizen
Chopwell Citizen
Birtley Citizen
Felling Citizen
Pharmacist, Raygales, Whickham
Head of Sexual Health Services Gateshead PCT
Gateshead Citizen
Connexions Advisor
Highfield Community Centre, Youth Worker
Gateshead Citizen
Chlamydia Screening Co-ordinator
STAG Gateshead Gay / Bisexual Men's Group
Gateshead Citizen
Gateshead Citizen
Bensham 'Visible' BME Group
Young People at Youth Offending Team Felling
Student Support Worker Gateshead College
Gateshead Citizen
Gateshead Citizen
Gateshead Citizen
Gateshead Young Women's Outreach Project
Body Positive N.E Worker
Gateshead Citizen
Team Leader NECA
Newcastle Health Promotion for Sex Workers, Worker
Gateshead Youth Council Manager
Youth and Community Learning Manager
Shabina Sadiq FPA
Peter Carter Department of Health
Jennie Winhall RED
Catherine Dennison Department of Health
Anne Graney Government Office North East
Nicole Stone Centre for Sexual Health Research
Advisory Group
Steering Group
Gateshead Citizens Street Interviews
One to One 'Real Story' Interviews
PCT: Primary Care Trust
SHA: Strategic Health Authority

# Our Cyborg Future?

Where am I? How am I? Who am I?

## Plug-in care

From cyborgs and high-tech clothing to mind-reading computers: is this really the future we want? Designers are creating a world in which every object, every building and every body is connected to a network. These changes blur the difference between natural and artificial, mind and body, you and the world.

We did not set out to design such an outcome. It's just happening – or it will, if we let it. The penetration of technology onto and into our bodies is happening without discussion of its consequences.

But it's not a plot. There's no Dr Frankenstein out there. This exhibition, curated by Andrew Caleya Chetty with Sabine Seymour for Dott 07 and the Discovery Museum, contained only real-life, practical and well-meant enhancements by dedicated designers and engineers.

The problem is that these experts tend to work in isolation from each other. They seldom get to stand back and talk with us about consequences and the bigger picture.

It's not an either/or discussion that we require – technology can be a boon if you've been disabled by accident or illness – but we do need to discuss priorities. The poorest nations spend $11 per person on health, compared with nearly $5,000 for every US citizen.

## How did Our Cyborg Future work?

Is this the way we want to live? A Dott 07 team pondered this as part of Our Cyborg Future. A programme of discussions and workshops across the North East culminated in an exhibition between 10 August and 27 October 2007 at the Victorian Great Hall in Newcastle's Discovery Museum – the main science museum for the North East of England. The exhibition was followed up by three special Cyborg debates during the Dott 07 Festival.

This project formed part of North East England's world-class festival and events programme.

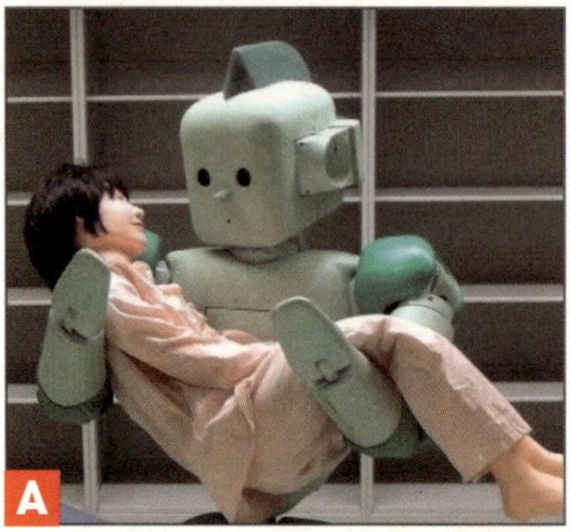


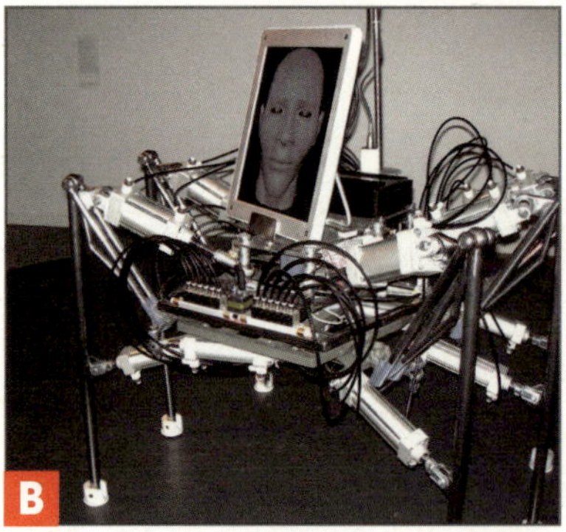


**A:** a Japanese-led research team has announced the creation of a robot that can carry human beings and is 'aimed at helping care for the country's growing number of elderly'. The RI-MAN robot can hear, see, smell, talk and touch, and is designed to be a partner robot that can carry out welfare and care tasks. The idea is grotesque – but a boom in assistive technology is on the way, whether we want it or not. Tech companies and researchers have identified a market among elderly people's children, who would rather pay for care than provide it in person. But will those who are supposed to benefit from such products be allowed to participate in the development of the technology?

**B:** the renowned Australian artist Stelarc demonstrated and performed this extraordinary 'Walking Head' – a six-legged walking robot – as a joint activity between Dott and Newcastle's celebrated Centre for Life

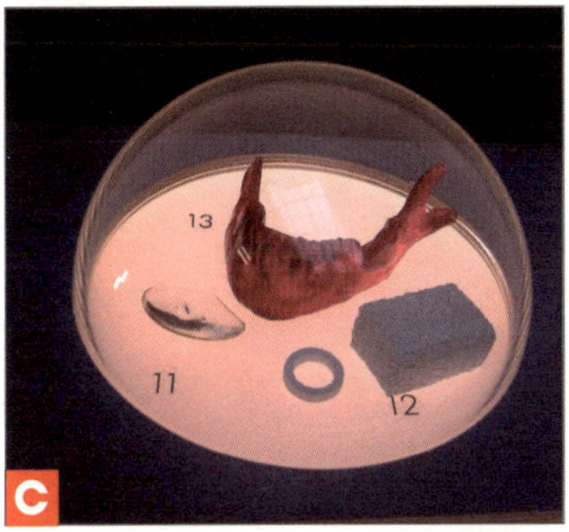


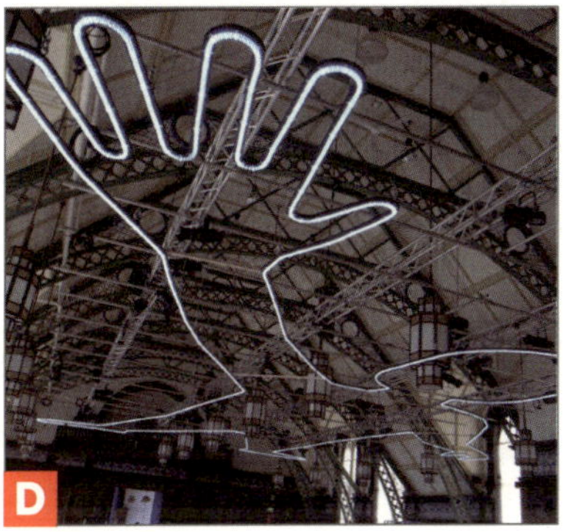

**C:** Tobie Kerridge, Ian Thompson and Nikki Stott – Biojewellery. Making jewellery special to you is hard to do, but how about jewellery made from your loved ones? One couple's cells were seeded onto a 'bioactive scaffold', which encouraged the cells to divide and grow rapidly. The resulting tissue took on the form of the scaffold, in this case a ring shape

**D:** this flying human form, designed by Land Design, the exhibition's designers, represented the blurring boundaries between the human form and a growing number of man-made spare body parts and enhancements

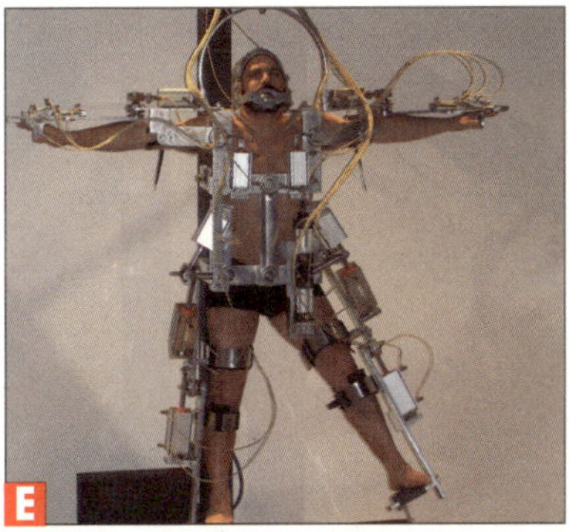

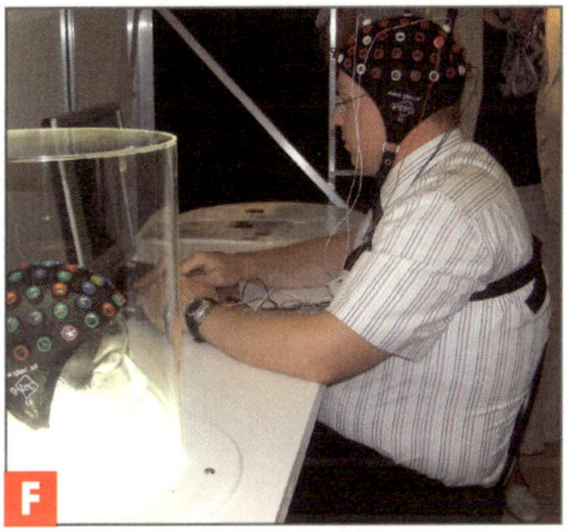

**E:** Marcel·lí Antúnez Roca – Requiem. The Requiem exoskeleton is made of aluminium sheets, stainless steel and 19 pneumatic pistons, enabling movement of the knees, thighs, groin, hip, shoulders, elbows, jaw and hands

**F:** G-Tec – Brain-Computer Interface for Computer Control. Wouldn't it be great to just have to 'think' to move a cursor on a computer screen? The Brain-Computer Interface aims to do this. A neuro-cap with sensors attached, which is linked to a computer, picks up mental activity and then detects changes and transforms them into a control signal

## What next?

If you would like to find out more about the impact of technology on our bodies and health, visit: www.dott07.com/go/cyborg

Below is a further list of useful websites and recommended background reading related to Our Cyborg Future:

**Android World**
www.androidworld.com

**Andy's Wearable Computing Resource**
Investigating wearable computers and associated technologies
www.redwoodhouse.com/wearable

**bionow**
Cluster support group of England's biotechnology, pharmaceutical and healthcare industry in the North West
www.bionow.co.uk

**Fashionable Technology™ Research Consortium**
www.fashionabletechnology.org

**Smart Textiles network**
Think-tank exploring the future of smart textiles, intelligent clothing, products and environments in the context of future markets
www.smartextiles.co.uk

**medGadget**
Internet journal of emerging medical technologies
www.medgadget.com

# Food: the ultimate design challenge?

Food is a crucial energy challenge. For a Northern city such as Toronto, 30% or more of its ecological footprint can be traced to its food systems[22]. From farm to plate, depending on the degree to which it has been processed, a typical food item may embody input energy between four and more than 100 times the food energy that enters our bodies[23].

## Food for thought

Global food systems are not sustainable. Industrialised food can consume over 100 times more energy in production and distribution than enters our bodies as nutrition. In developed countries, the food consumption of a single family generates eight tonnes of $CO_2$ emissions a year[24]. This madness is enabled by non-renewable fossil fuel. But what to do?

Over the past 10 years, the growing number of food miles and escalating $CO_2$ emissions from the transportation of foods alone have fuelled greater demand for locally grown food. But, for many of us who live in cities, the separation between city and country has seemed to be an obstacle to local food production.

Some planners and architects have responded by discussing new ways to grow food in cities in what they call 'continuous productive urban landscapes', building on existing resources such as the UK's 59 city farms, nearly 1,000 community gardens and 66 school farms. The focus of the Dott 07 food projects was to re-frame food systems as design opportunities, and to consider what design steps we might take to make it easier for city dwellers to grow their own fruit and vegetables.

The Urban Farming project in Middlesbrough brought together more than 1,000 citizens – or 'New Urban Farmers' – to grow food in small, medium and large containers all over town.

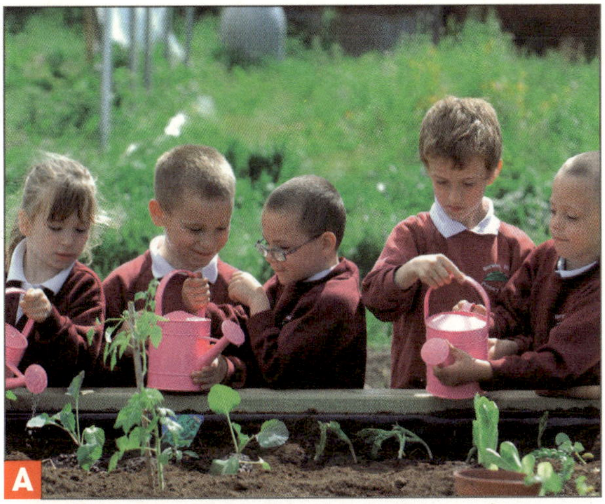

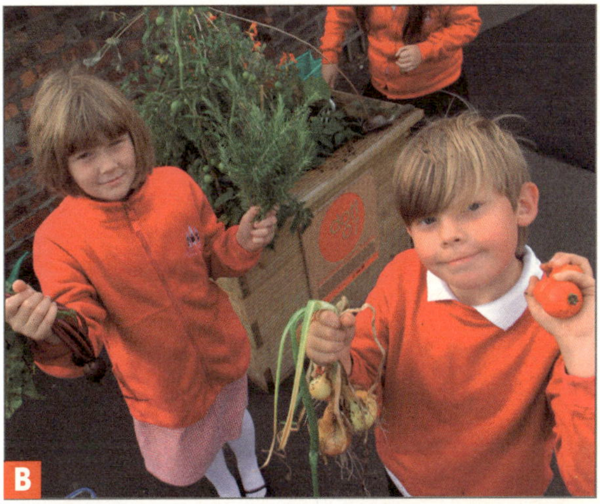

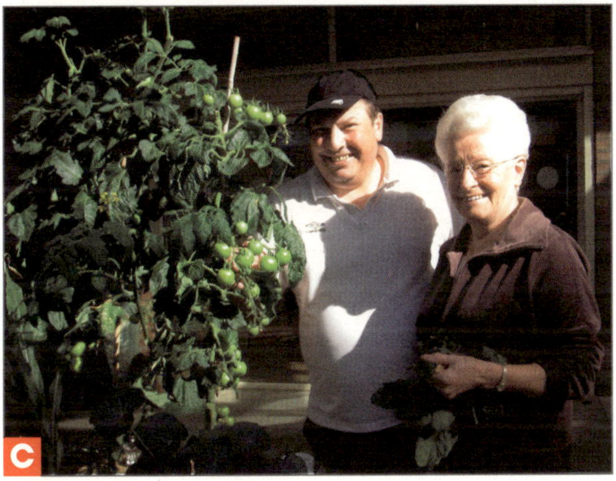

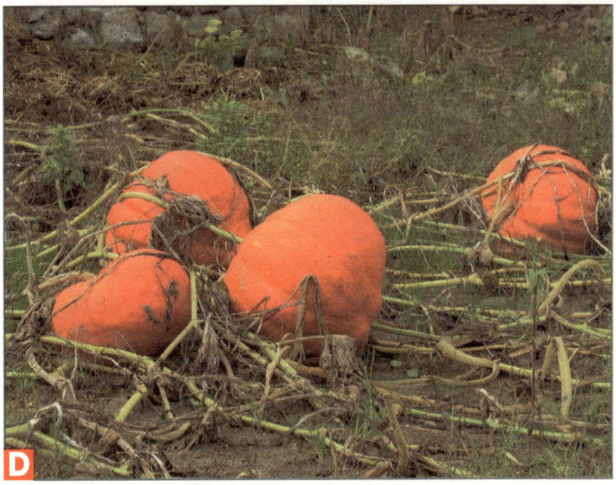

# How might we keep food within city limits – from farm to plate?

Up to a quarter of the ecological footprint of towns and cities is made up of the way food is grown, distributed, prepared, eaten – and chucked away[25]. What practical design steps might change that?

**A:** schoolchildren planting at Berwick Allotments as part of the Urban Farming project
**B:** students from Linthorpe Community Primary School bring in their harvest for the town meal
**C:** Jimmy Cooper and Pat Hindmarch, members of the Middlesbrough Neighbourhood Trust gardening club
**D:** red pumpkins

PHOTOS: A & B – North News and Pictures; C – Dot 07; D – Steve Messam

## Growing together

During the summer and autumn of 2007, thousands of people living and working in Middlesbrough participated in a project to increase local food production and reduce food miles.

Along the way, young, old, rich and poor worked together, growing food and realising new relationships with local food producers and existing growers in the town and its surrounding area. Their goal has been to pioneer a new sustainable future – not just for Middlesbrough, but also other post-industrial communities across the UK.

They were also working to raise awareness of the benefits of and opportunities for growing and securing food for our towns and cities. Local growers need to be connected to existing and new markets, a new relationship needs to be struck between urban and rural, and communities need inspirational and educational 'soil to plate' experiences.

Middlesbrough Council and David Barrie, senior producer for Dott 07, have led the project, working in close partnership with Groundwork South Tees, Middlesbrough Primary Care Trust, more than 15 primary and secondary schools, many local community and voluntary sector organisations, and existing allotment growers in the town. It was driven by Bioregional's commitment to the concept of one planet living, developed in collaboration with the World Wildlife Fund and endorsed by the Minister of State for the Environment, Food and Rural Affairs.

**When you eat an iceberg lettuce from the US, 127 calories of energy are used in its shipping and merchandising for every one calorie of nutrition that enters your mouth[26]**

**There are 52 transport and process stages involved in making one bottle of ketchup[27]**

**Figure 1: Schematic of the supply chain of a can of cola and its proportional carbon footprint (illustrative)**

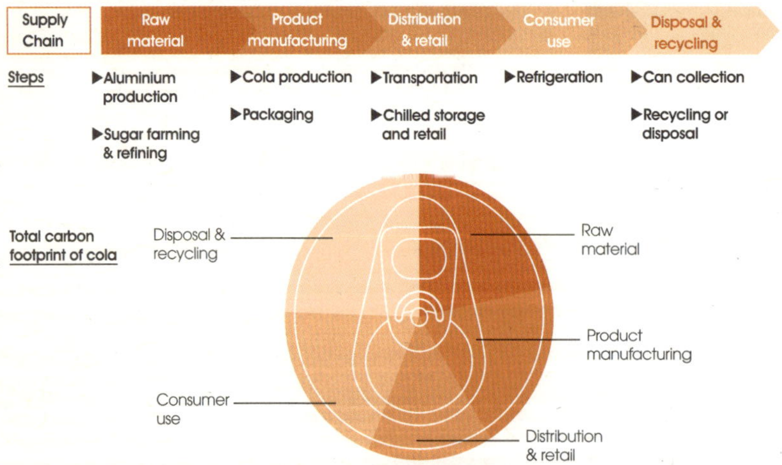


PIE CHART: "Carbon footprints in the supply chain" Carbon Trust Report CT616, 2007

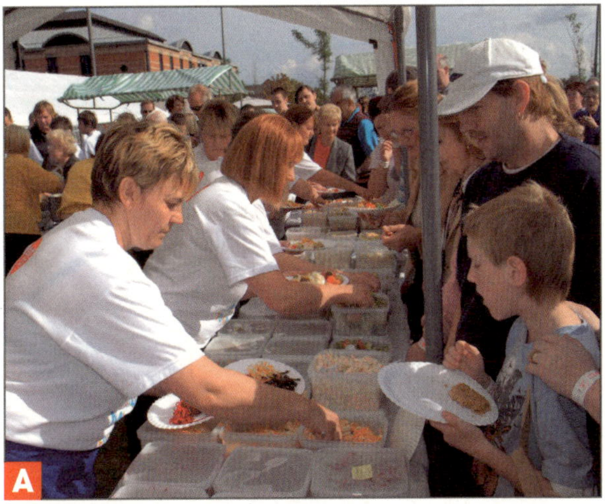

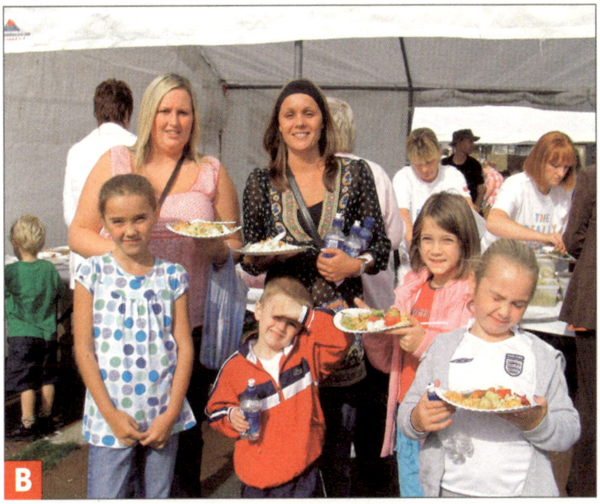

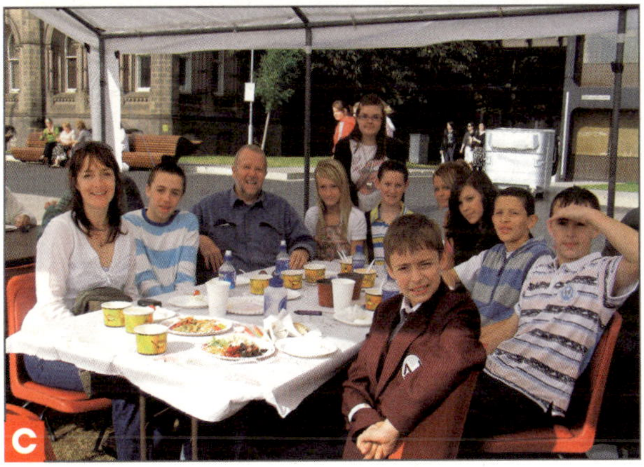

**A:** lunch is served to 1,500 people at the Middlesbrough town meal
**B:** Emma Thomas, community health development lead at East Middlesbrough for Middlesbrough Primary Care Trust, and Donna Siviter, school nurse assistant for Middlesbrough Primary Care Trust with children from Brambles Farm Community Centre and Brambles Farm School
**C:** teachers and growers from MacMillan Academy
**D:** Anthony Kirkbridge, study support for Middlesbrough schools, with courgettes grown in schools across Middlesbrough

PHOTO: A – North News and Pictures

### How did Urban Farming work?

Between October 2006 and March 2007, senior producer David Barrie and his team consulted community groups, voluntary organisations, schools and public health organisations in Middlesbrough. Barrie was supported by Zest Innovation, a North East based service design consultancy, and Debra Solomon, artist and author of culiblog.com, an online publication about food culture.

More than 80 groups, schools and other organisations expressed an interest in participating in a 'soil to table' project devoted to finding a healthier, more sustainable local food system. These included primary and secondary schools, pre-school groups (Sure Start), residential homes, allotment associations, mental health units in local hospitals, residents' groups, voluntary organisations and even the staff of a smart department store in a main shopping street in the town centre. The local council chipped in by agreeing to dig up part of the main local park so the Urban Farming teams could grow specialist plants and food there.

The groups identified locations in which to grow food and the produce they would like to cultivate. Then, in May 2007, about 1,000 people began growing fruit and vegetables in containers at locations across the town. They received support from local horticulturalists, allotment growers, farmers and food producers.

Between June and September, this new team of urban farmers brought their harvested ingredients to a 'kitchen playground' event: three week-long blocks of activity in which people prepared, cooked and ate dishes based on ingredients that they had grown themselves.

The frenzy of food production culminated in September in a 'Meal for Middlesbrough' – a banquet for 1,500 in the town's main square. Participants in the growing project created the menu from produce they'd harvested. Local producers provided meat and vegetables to supplement the meal, which was cooked and eaten in the open air.

Finally, several containers grown in Middlesbrough were presented at the Dott 07 Festival and participating groups prepared food for visitors in a special-edition kitchen playground.

**Figure 1: Average ecological footprint for the city of Toronto**

- **23.9%** Transportation
- **20.9%** Housing
- **31.9%** Food
- **17.7%** Products & services
- **5.6%** Waste

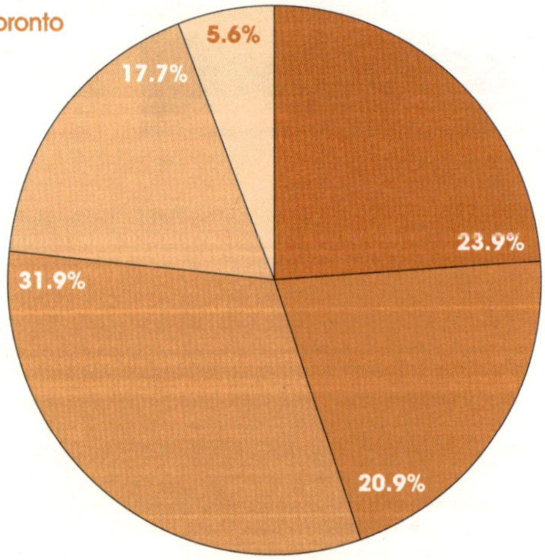


Toronto, in Ontario, Canada, has high transportation and housing contributions to its ecological footprint, but by far the biggest factor is food, at 31.9%. The chart opposite is measuring the average ecological footprint as being equal to 5.30 hectares.

PIE CHART: The Environmental Impact Assessment & Policy Development Office, Toronto

## Why Middlesbrough?

'Like lots of post-industrial towns and cities, Middlesbrough has plenty of surplus land,' explains David Barrie. 'A certain proportion can be redeveloped for commercial use, but there is still a lot of surplus space. The town has done amazing things over the past two years in improving its public realm, so why not turn some of it into a different form of public space?'

Industrially, too, the area is evolving fast. Areas to the north of Middlesbrough in Teesside were the heartland of Britain's heavy chemical industries. Now the area is diversifying into renewables and biofuel production, most recently via a £250million investment from Ensus for Britain's biggest bioethanol plant.

'The area is going to play a part in our future, more environmentally based economy,' says Barrie, 'and there are many people in Middlesbrough who care passionately about their town. It's a good place to do a public project.'

## What next?

Over the next year, the urban farming project will build on its successes so far:

- Mapping locations where food is grown already
- Mapping sites or 'edible landscapes' where food growing could be extended
- Deploying planters to individuals and groups around the city
- Designing kitchen playgrounds and staging a town meal.

Middlesbrough Council commissioned a map from designers Andre Viljoen and Katrina Bohn – authors of *Continuous Productive Urban Landscapes* – which identifies existing and prospective food-growing sites in Middlesbrough (see 82/83). It details existing allotments in the town, maps surplus land and highlights connections between the town and local food producers. This is a plan for the local authority and others to consider as a new context for strategies towards a more local and sustainable food economy.

The team behind the project is listed on pages 96 to 99. For more information go to: www.dott07.com/go/urbanfarming

Below: when French scientist Jean-Marc Jancovici added up all the processes called on to produce the food eaten (in France), the total was about a third of all French emissions

| The carbon costs of food | Million tonnes equivalent |
|---|---|
| Direct emissions from agriculture | 42.0 |
| Fertiliser manufacturing | 0.8 |
| Road transport for goods | 4.0 |
| Road transport for people | 1.0 |
| Truck manufacture and diesel oil refining | 0.8 |
| Store heating | 0.4 |
| Electricity | 0.7 |
| Packaging production | 1.5 |
| Methane emissions from food waste | 1.0 |
| **Total** | **52.2** |
| National emissions (CEMA) | 171.0 |
| % emissions linked to food | 30% |

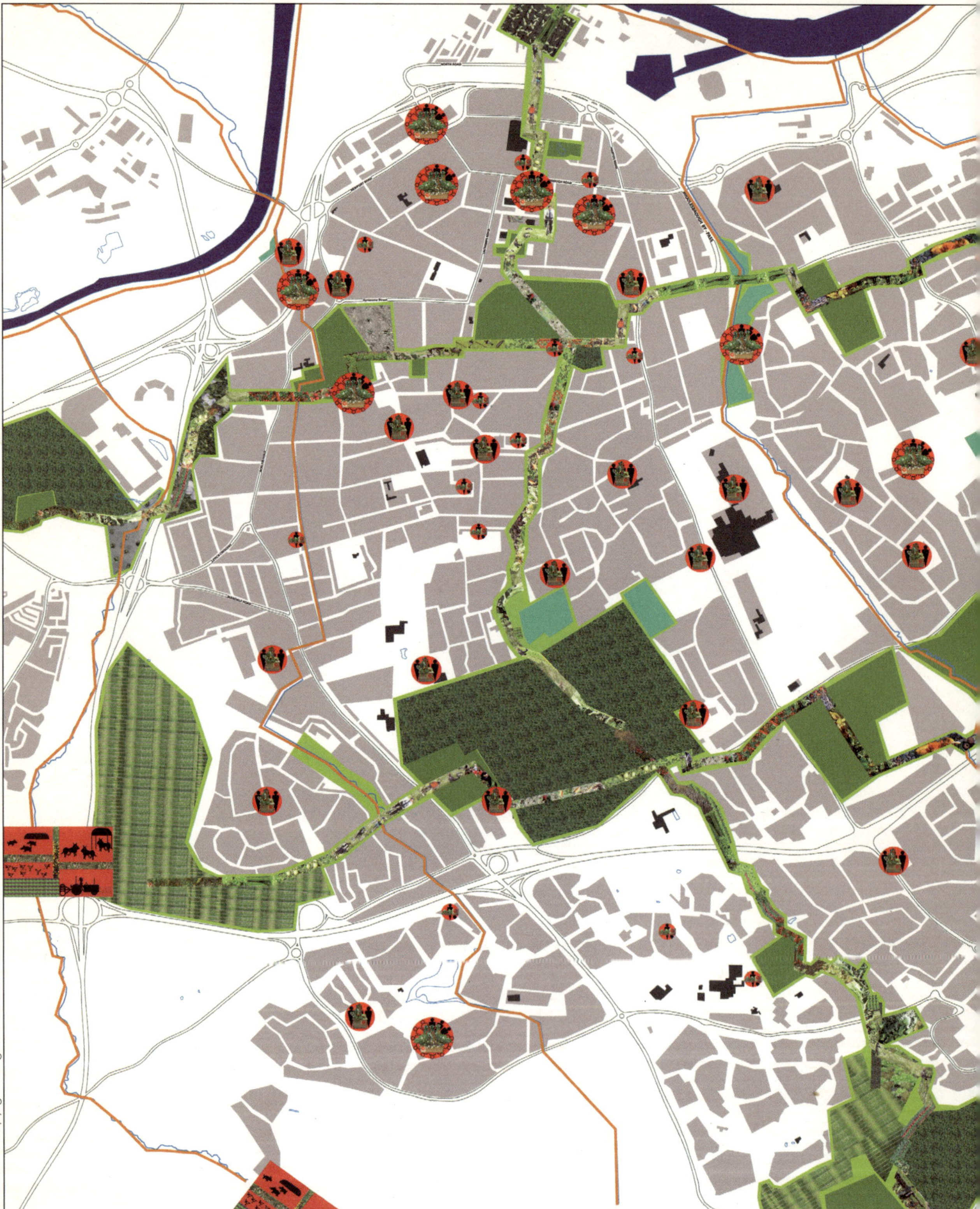

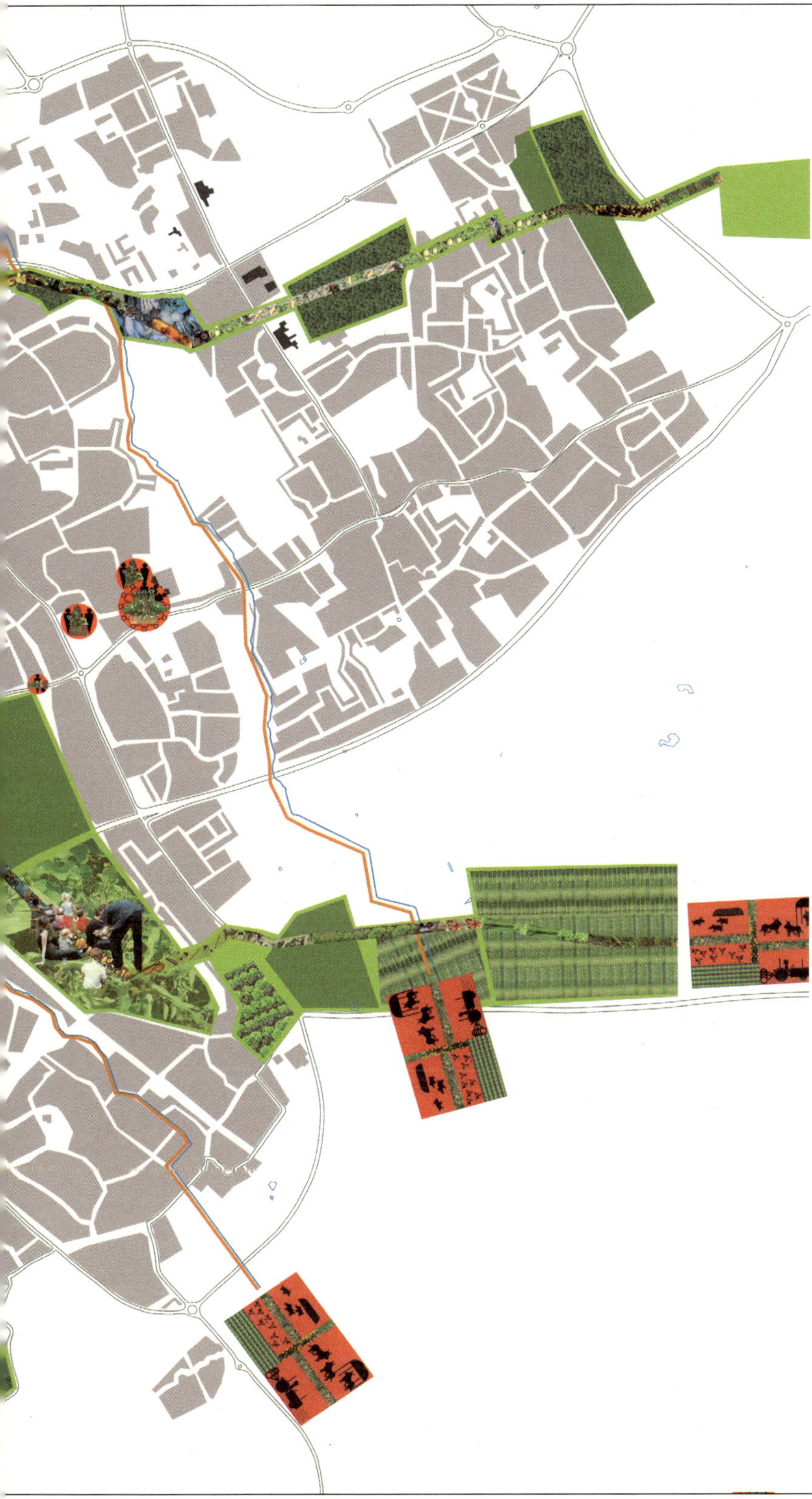

**DOTT 07 Small containers**
136 Window boxes and barrels were distributed as urban farming containers, looked after by individuals and organisations.

**DOTT 07 Medium containers**
68 medium containers, one meter square in area, were used for growing fruit and vegetables, these were looked after by schools, service providers, community organisations and at visitor attractions.

**DOTT 07 Large containers**
48 large containers, four square meters in area, were farmed by schools, community centres and other organisations.

**MIMA and the Parks Department**
looked after an extensive urban farming area alongside the city's revitalised Cental Gardens. This site, completely open to the public, produced a remarkable crop for Middlesbrough's celebratory Town Meal.

**Left:** more than 1,000 citizens grew food in small, medium and large containers all over town as part of Dott 07. The success of this experiment prompted Middlesbrough to commission this map of 'edible landscapes' by Andrew Viljoen and Katrina Bohn. The map shows where food growing could be extended in the future. The design challenge now is to create services, markets and infrastructures that will help Middlesbrough become self-sufficient in food once again.

# Urban Space Station: space-age rooftop urban greenhouse

Reducing food miles and using far less energy to grow food means producing more food in the cities where most of us live. As we found with our Urban Farming project in Middlesbrough, there are many under-used allotments and plots to start with. But in dense downtown areas, where land is scarce, we also need to grow food on rooftops.

The proposal behind this project was to build, install and unveil the world's first rooftop urban greenhouse atop a building near the Dott 07 Festival. The Urban Space Station (USS) design team is led by Natalie Jeremijenko, Visiting Global Distinguished Professor, College of Arts and Sciences, New York University.

The Urban Space Station is designed to generate its own energy and can provide energy to the building it rests upon. USS is designed to use the $CO_2$-enriched air produced by people and machines in a building via the output of the heating, ventilation and air conditioning (HVAC) system. The USS adapts closed-system design developed for space stations to an urban agriculture facility optimised for the unique constraints of an urban green roof. It couples open ecological systems with closed-systems engineering. This mutualistic host/parasite relationship increases $CO_2$ fixation and waste air cycling.

Green roofs are relatively new and are perhaps the final frontier of urban space. They are being colonised at an alarming rate for their promised energy conservation benefits as well as other environmental services such as urban agriculture.

Unfortunately, it did not prove possible to install a prototype for Dott 07 – but we hope to do so for Dott 09. For more information visit: www.nyu.edu/projects/xdesign/uss

**A&B:** the design team's impressions of how the urban greenhouses might look situated on rooftop spaces in the city

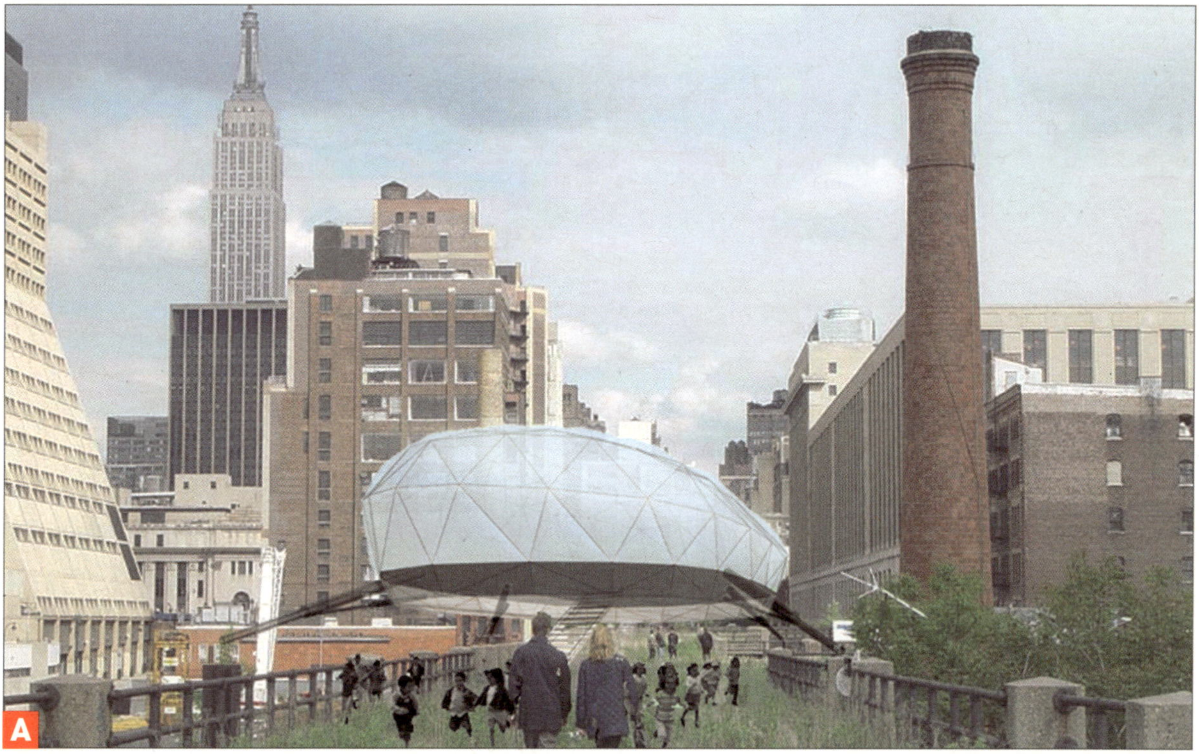

A

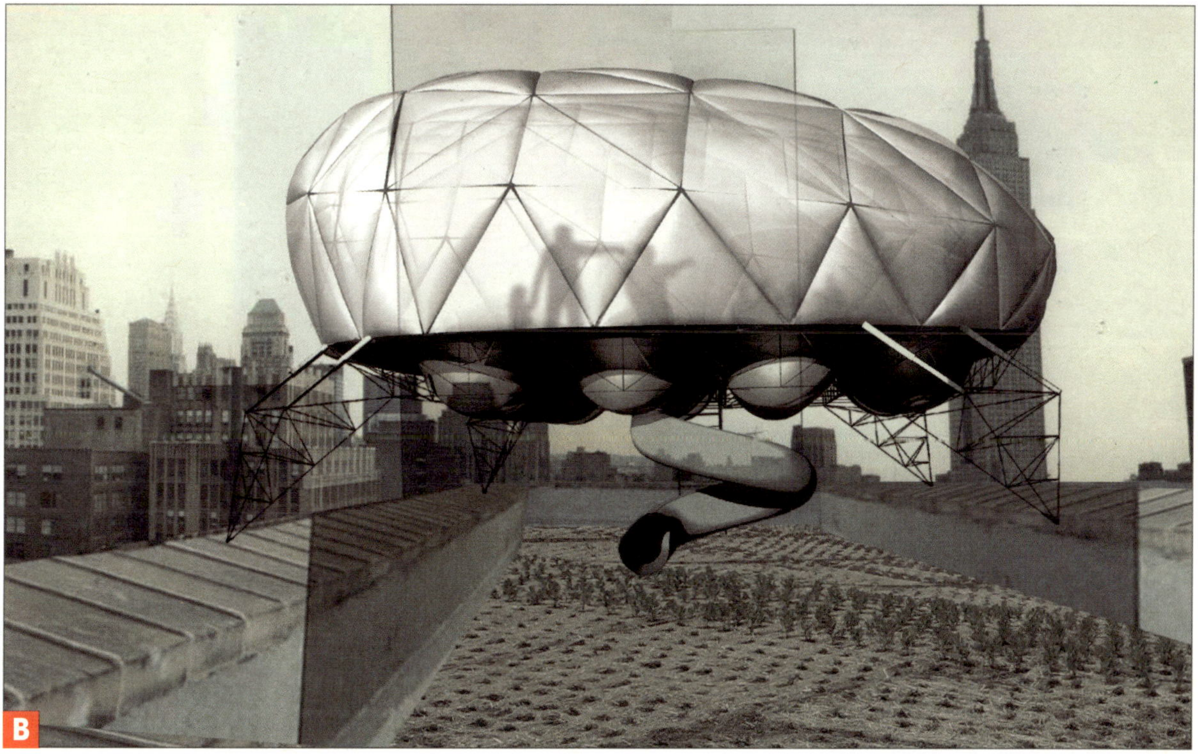

B

ILLUSTRATIONS: Open Source Space – Angel Borrego, Fran Gallardo and Natalie Jeremijenko

# Tyne Salmon Trail

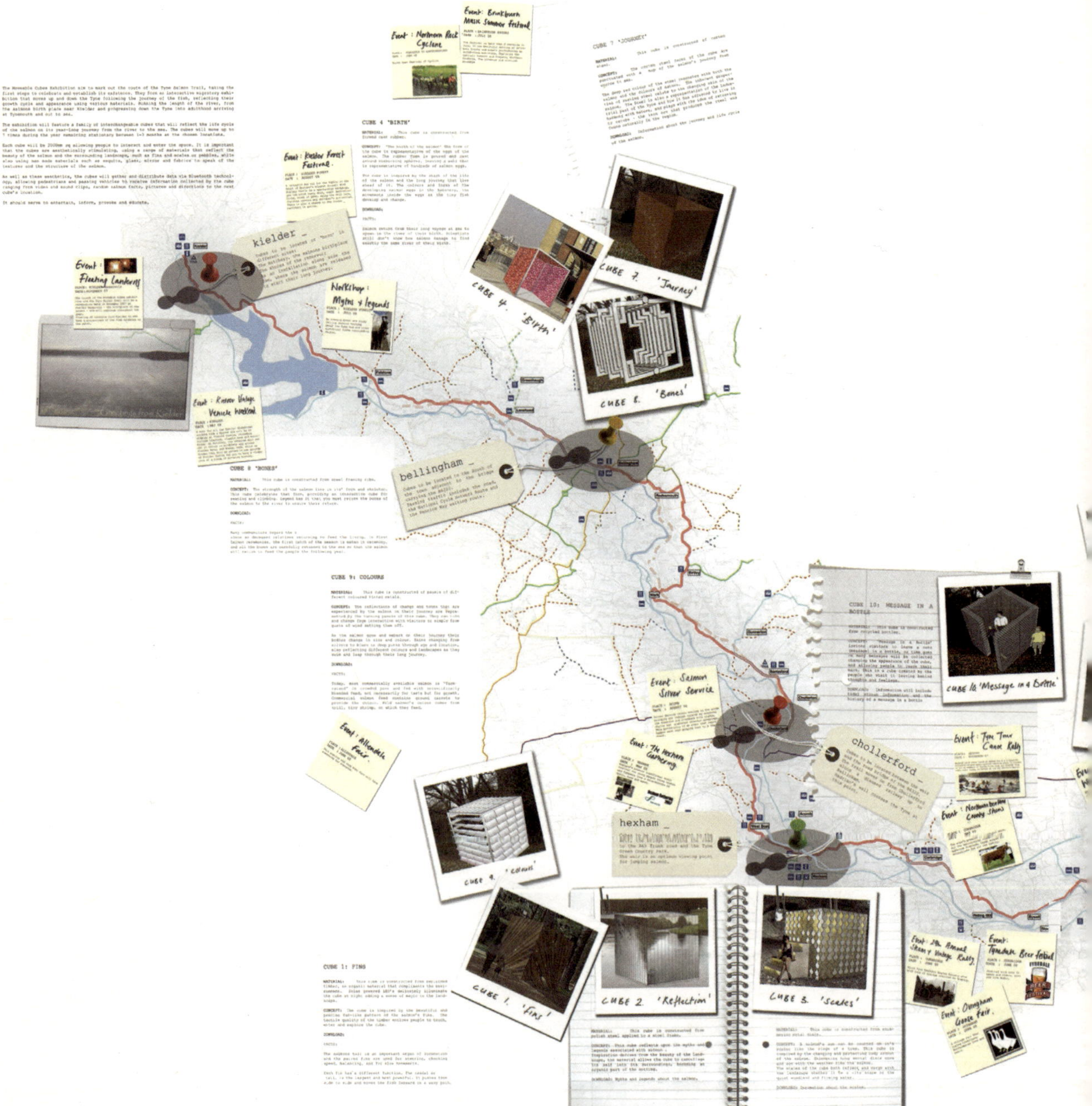

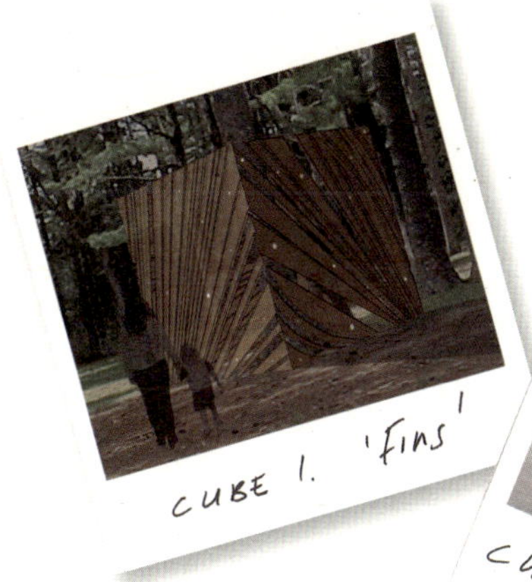


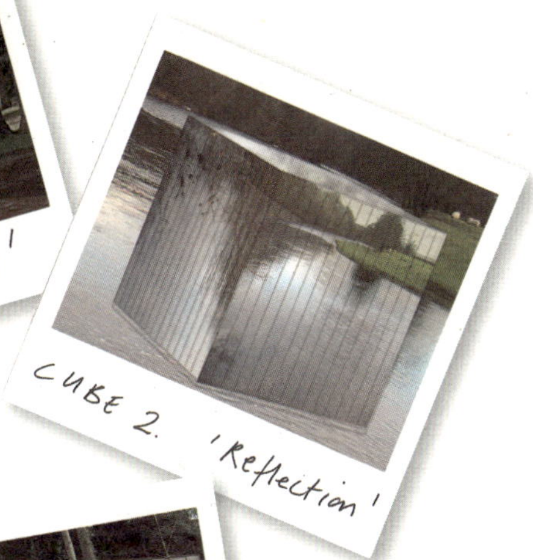


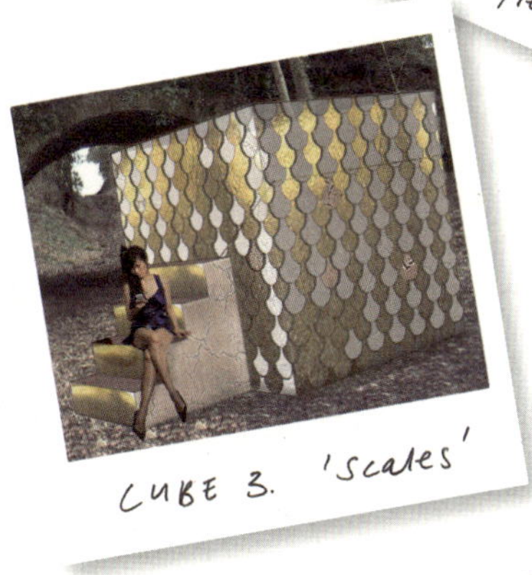


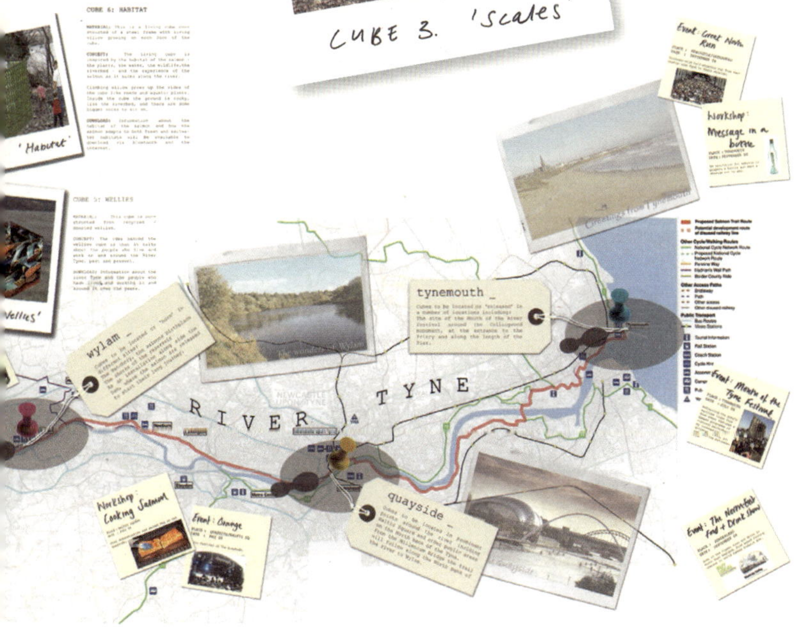


MAP: xsite architecture

The Tyne Salmon Trail project celebrates the River Tyne, its heritage and its diverse ecosystem. It explores low-impact ways to improve access to the River Tyne and its different species.

Ross Lowrie, senior officer at the Environment Agency and the project leader, worked with architects xsite to create a trail following the salmon from their birthplace at Kielder, down to the sea at Tynemouth and back again to Kielder where they return to spawn and die.

To enhance visitor experience, the team conceived the Moveable Cubes Exhibition: installations were posted at points along the salmon trail and three events were held whose aim was to trigger memories for people and encourage communities to engage with the river in diverse, unusual ways.

The Environment Agency was keen to harness the power of public art and technology to promote awareness of environmental issues, our changing landscape and, in particular, the river.

Good design and good public art engages people and makes them remember a place. Commissions North have now asked xsite to take the idea forward.

The trail serves to entertain, inform, provoke and educate. The cubes (inset) gather and distribute data via Bluetooth technology, allowing pedestrians and passing vehicles to receive information by the cubes ranging from videos and sound recordings to random salmon facts, pictures and directions to the next cube

# Design Event 07: still a role for designers of things?

Founded by Karen Stone, Design Event is the North East's first annual design festival. Conceived in 2005 from a small shopfront on Pink Lane in Newcastle, the festival originated with a group of local designers who wanted to put on exhibitions and shout about what was happening in the region. Since then, the festival has grown to become a region-wide delight and, this year, is supported by Dott 07.

The core of Design Event is a celebration of design in all its forms, including graphics, product, fashion, illustration and architecture. It aims to provide a platform to showcase the high quality of design talent emerging from the region, alongside designers of national and international acclaim.

The festival's success lies in its mix of design disciplines, the unfailing enthusiasm and innovation of the North East region's design community and the continued alliance to its grassroots origins.

With growth comes the confidence and passion to keep the festival feeling fresh and vibrant year after year. With that in mind, Design Event have chosen to focus on a specific theme each year.

A

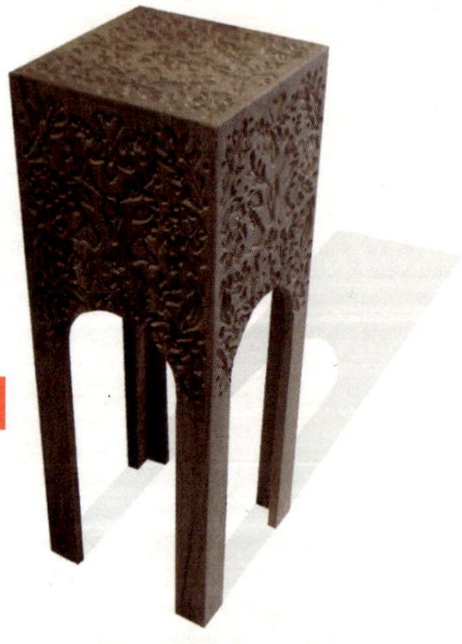

## Design Event 07

**The theme for Design Event 07 was 'How do we want to live?'**

- In an urban environment, how can we escape and find solace?
- How can we create and add more value to the things we buy so that we treasure them, rather than discard them as soon as the next trend comes along?
- How often do we take time to look up and appreciate what's around us?

The curatorial team of Karen Stone and Danielle Pender produced a programme incorporating exhibitions that responded to the theme from both a sustainable and a North East-pride focus. The event also featured a series of talks in association with the National Endowment for Science, Technology and the Arts (NESTA), which was aimed at kick-starting a year-round programme of talks, events and discussions.

This project formed part of North East England's world-class festival and events programme. For more information, visit: www.design-event.co.uk

A: Launch 2007, Walnut Rejse by Polly Walnut
B: Launch 2007, David Irwin
C: Contains, Sunday newspaper cut out

B

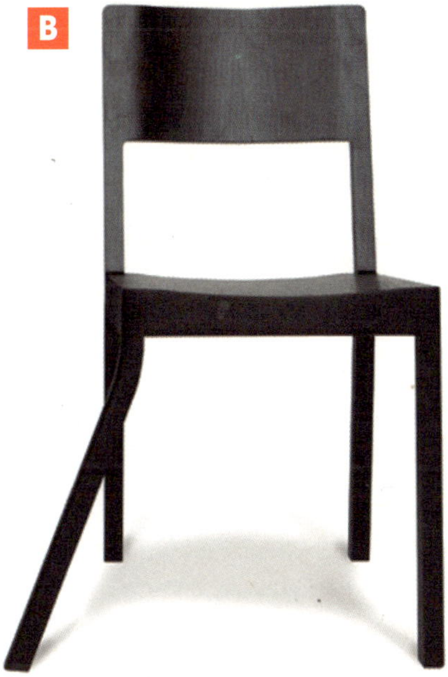

C

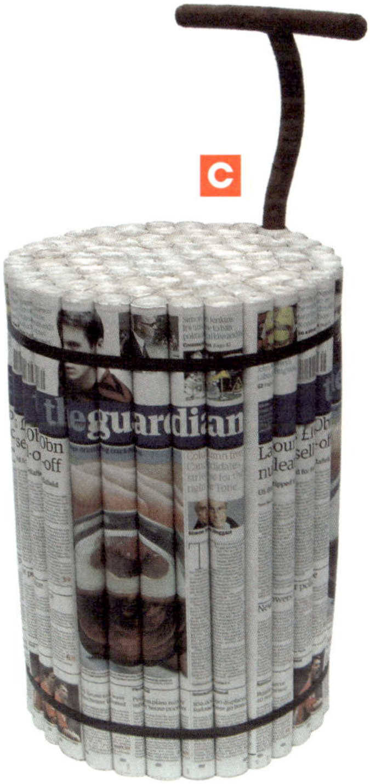


*'There's definitely a buzz in Newcastle around design at the moment, with individuals really making things happen. Design Event is a great way for designers to develop professionally and get their work seen. We need to encourage and support design entrepreneurs, and that's exactly what Design Event is doing for the North East'*

Wayne Hemingway, designer

## Design Event highlights

**One-Off Factory**
This series of exhibitions across Sunderland explored the creation of prototypes for our future selves: designs that propose an alternative way of thinking or living. Each project asked how design can find unorthodox solutions to familiar problems, from the furniture we use to forms of micro-architecture. Designers produced one-off works for the show, using it as a forum for experimentation and testing their ideas in public. Featured designers include Mathias Bengtsson, N55 and Max Lamb.

**From the Earth We Came...**
This project placed new work by illustrators Daisy de Villeneuve, Lucy Mclauchlan and Steven Wilson throughout the streets of Newcastle Gateshead, curated by Platform Projects. The works invited passers-by to consider the way we live among the buildings that surround us. Through subtle design interventions and illustrations applied to the city's surfaces, the works highlighted intricate ornamental features and the colonisation of man-made structures by plants.

**Contains**
Curated by [re]design, Contains told the stories behind the products we use every day – the people who make them, the materials they use, the energy consumed, the miles travelled – in an innovative, inspiring and accessible exhibition showing how design can make a difference. Housed in a series of shipping containers in the retail heart of Newcastle, the venue complemented the exhibition's question of where things come from and what their true cost is.

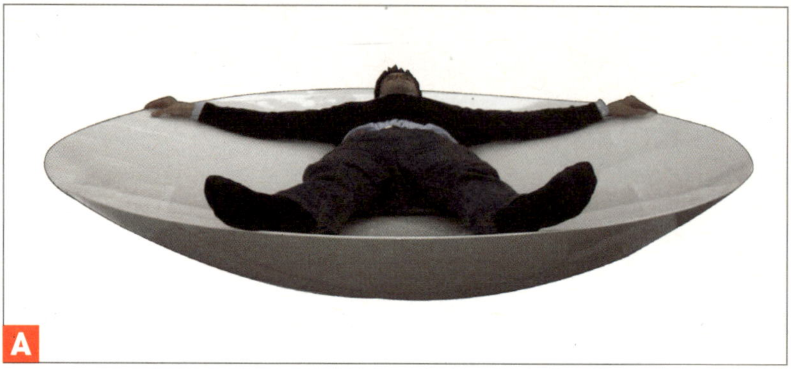

A

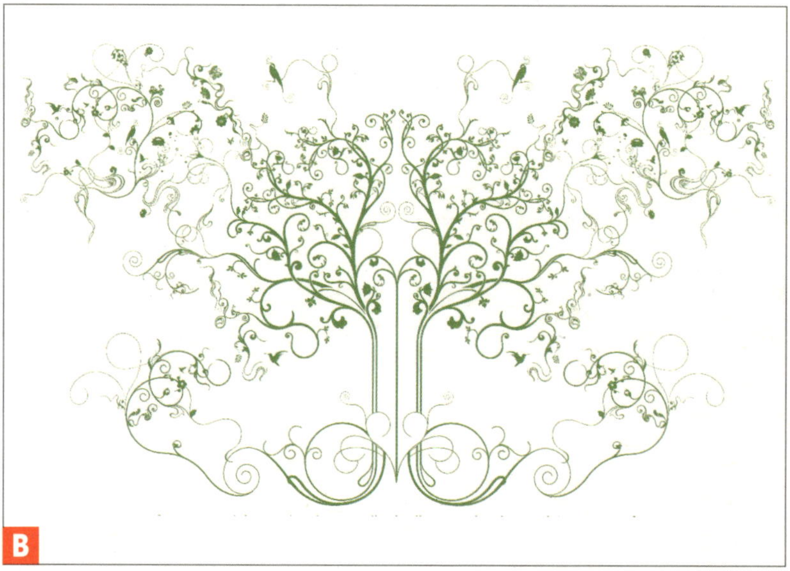

B

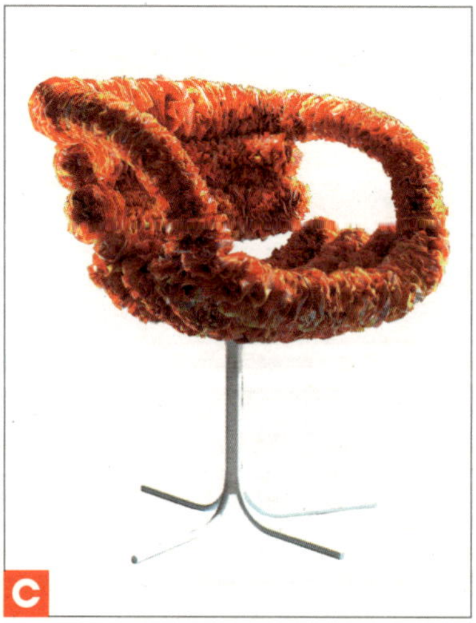

C

A: One-Off Factory
B: From the earth we came, Steven Wilson
C: Contains
D: Delight in Design
E: Build, Our Friends in the North
F: Plastics Recyling Factory
G: Design for Science, Virus Models

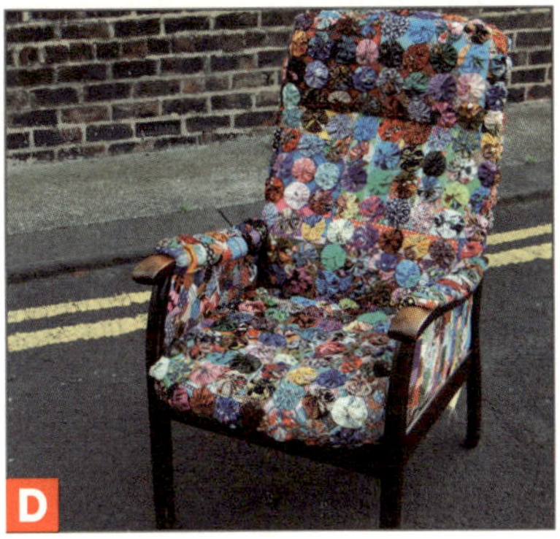
D

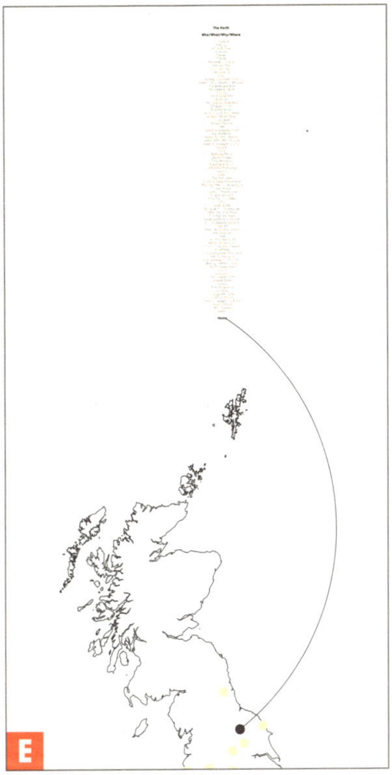
E

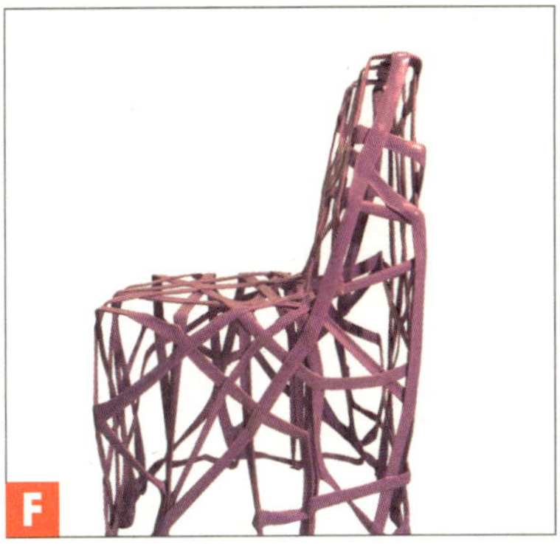
F

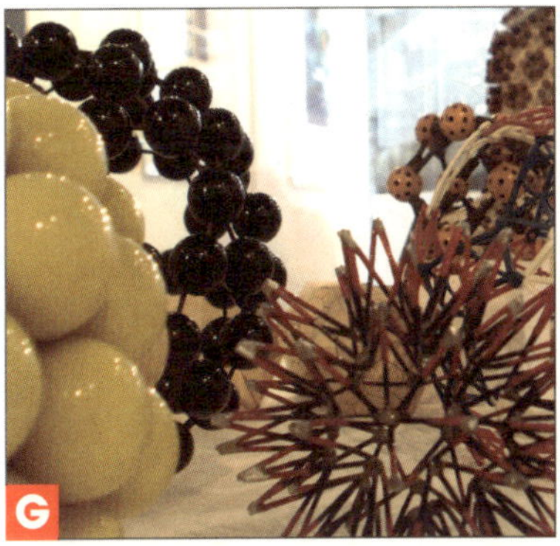
G

**Delight in Design**
Alistair Fuad-Luke worked with North East design forum Designed and Made to look at the process of design and how the beauty and joy of making can be celebrated. Where possible, locally-sourced, found, recycled or virgin materials were used and exhibited as a dinner party with a difference where the experience was of equal importance as the exhibits.

**Our Friends in the North**
Our Friends in the North traced the evolution of technique, process and training in graphic design between 1977 and 2007.

Acclaimed artists with roots in the North East, including Vaughan Oliver, Build and Richard Fenwick, were commissioned to produce a new piece of work illustrating the impact of the North East on their creative style or working process. This was curated by the Lobster Foundation.

**Launch 2007**
Curated by Deadgood ltd, Launch is a maverick design exhibition held annually in Newcastle and was one of the founding elements of Design Event 05. Over the past three years, it has established itself as one of the North's biggest 3D design showcases and provides a launchpad for new products by regional designers. Held in venues as innovative as the products on show, this year Launch took place at Newcastle City Centre's decommissioned fire station.

**Plastics Recycling Factory**
You may put your newspapers, bottles and plastics into the recycling bin, but do you know what happens to them after that? At a series of performances, Cohda Design transformed household plastic packaging waste into innovative handmade seating designs.

Early designs from the process were a hit at New York's furniture fair earlier this year. Design Event 07 provided the first opportunity to see the process behind the work.

**Design4Science**
Design4Science highlighted the impact of design in communicating scientific breakthroughs and how new scientific advances have inspired designers from the post-war era to the present day. Curated by Shirley Wheeler at the University of Sunderland, it featured new commissions by Daniel Brown, Paul Cocksedge and Andy Altman.

It also included a post-war archive of drawings, models, and animation from the MRC Laboratory of Molecular Biology in Cambridge, designs produced for the 1951 Festival of Britain and the winning entries from the National Design4Science Student Design competition.

# Pecha Kucha

Pecha Kucha, Japanese for 'chit-chat', was founded in Tokyo in 2003 by Klein Dytham Architecture. Pecha Kucha nights have taken place in Berlin, New York, San Francisco, Los Angeles, London and Sydney – and Newcastle upon Tyne.

In December 2006 and May 2007, Dott 07 brought Pecha Kucha to Newcastle's Robert Stephenson Centre for a fast-paced evening of fun that featured a collection of inspirational images and stories by some of the most influential people in the creative industries. Karen Stone and Danielle Pender curated both nights.

At the Pecha Kucha nights, 10 to 12 speakers from design, architecture, art, music and photography each talked about 20 slides for 20 seconds each slide. There was no brief and images could be as obscure or as mundane as the speaker wished.

They ranged from things that inspire them – a holiday snap, their favourite books or football team – to something they hate.

The objective is to inspire through unconventional methods.

Among the many stars from the worlds of design, architecture, photography and the creative arts who took part were *Elle Decoration* 'Young Designer of the Year' Alexander Taylor; BAFTA award-winning art director Simon Sankarayya and Ross Millard, singer and guitarist from the Futureheads.

John Thackara, Dott 07's Programme Director and host for the evening, introduced the various speakers, saying: 'Dott 07 is about starting conversations instead of telling people how to live. One way to do this is setting up the Pecha Kucha event, where the only requirement is to talk about stuff.'

For more information, visit:
www.pecha-kucha.org

**A:** Pecha Kucha crowd in the Robert Stephenson Centre
**B:** John Thackara welcoming the Pecha Kucha crowd
**C:** warehouse roof of the Robert Stephenson Centre
**D:** Steve Messam, Fold Gallery
**E:** Françoise Lamy, Cinefeel
**F:** Tom Shakespeare

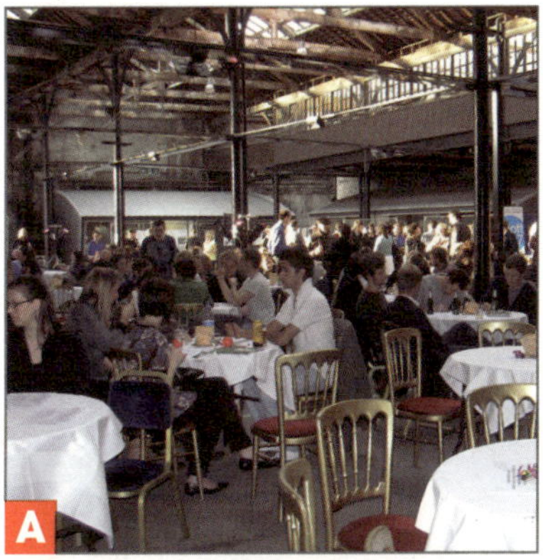
A

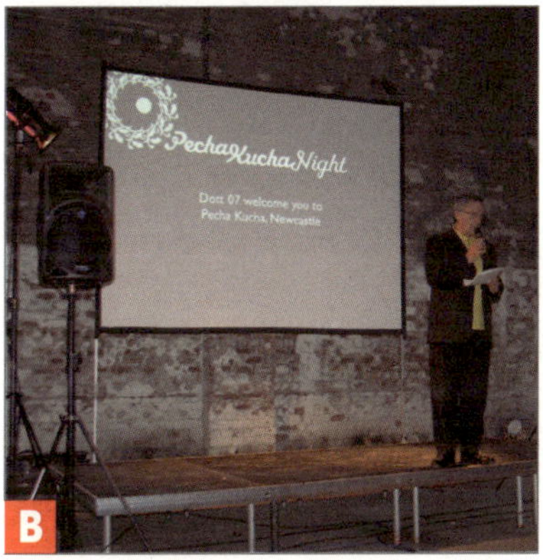

B

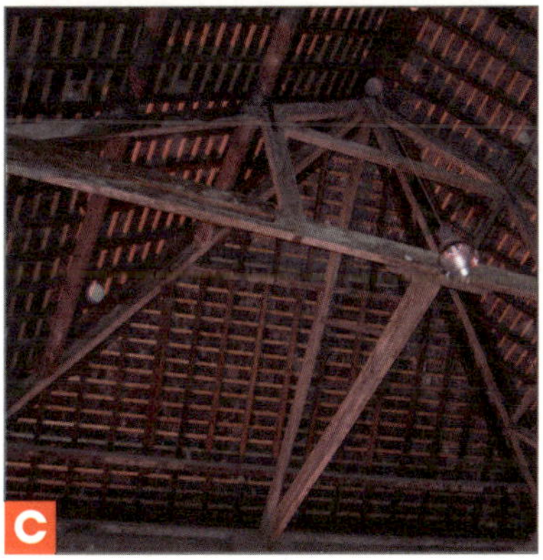
C

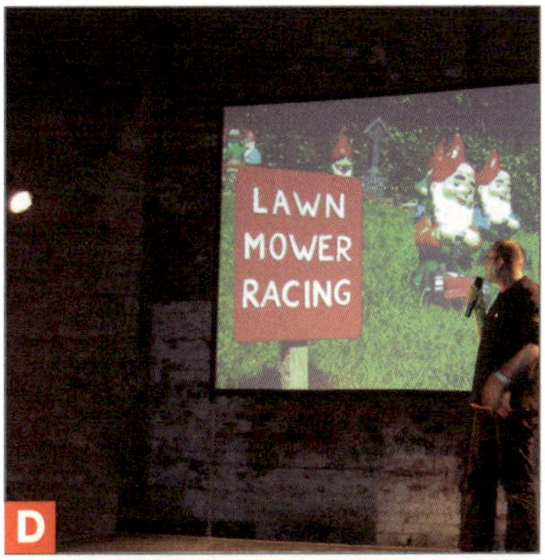

D

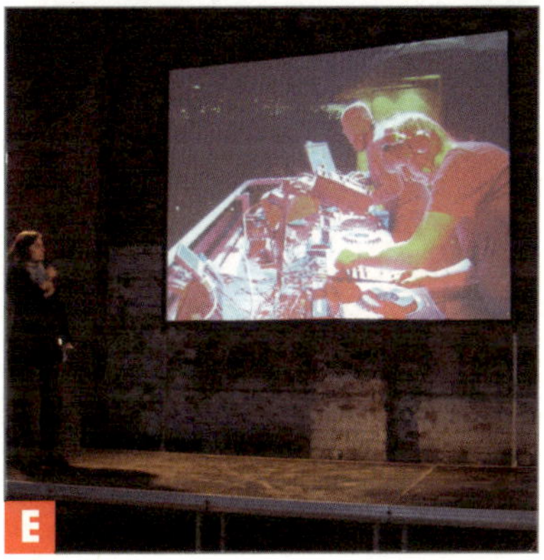
E

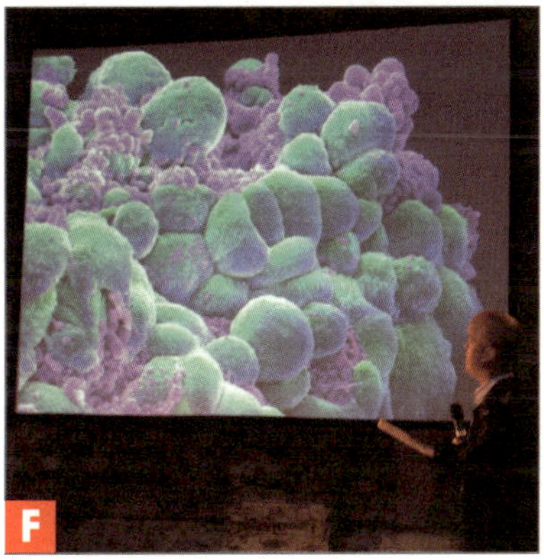
F

## D. Steve Messam, FRED and Fold Gallery

First up for the evening was the inimitable, charming and very, very creative Steve Messam. Artist in his own right and co-founder of FRED and Fold, Steve hit us hard with his fetish for red and round things.

## E. Françoise Lamy, Cinefeel

Françoise Lamy of Cinefeel has been curating and promoting the work of emerging directors, digital artists, VJs and new electronic music since 1994. She treated us to images from her travels to London, Beijing, Moscow, New Delhi and Saudi Arabia.

## F. Tom Shakespeare

Multi-talented author, academic and film-maker Tom Shakespeare took us on a journey through the metaphorical consequences of falling and laughing. Pictured is the startling image of breast cancer cells growing out of control.

**Pecha Kucha Night**
**G: Tania Marcetic**
**H: Alexander Taylor**

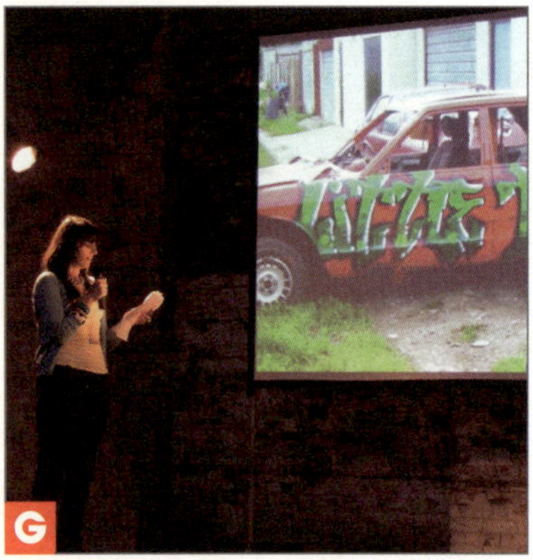
G

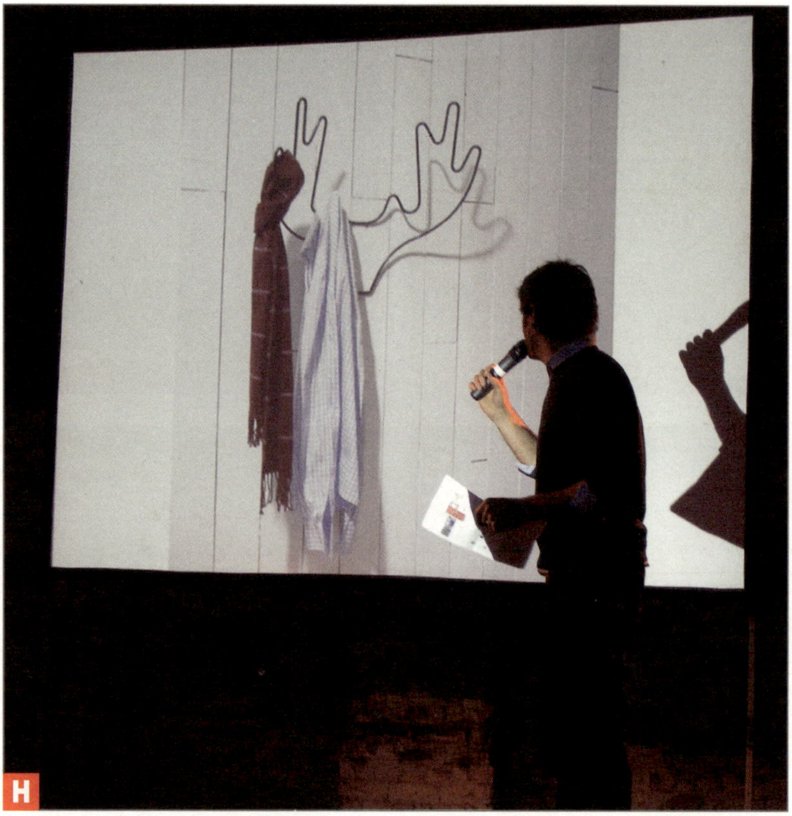
H

## G. Tania Marcetic

Tania Marcetic, a prize student at Northumbria University who received instant MySpace fame with her 'Everything Must Go' caravan, which appeared on 12 May for one day only. Her presentation took us through the bare, raw, urban, obscure and sometimes dingy images that inspire her work.

## H. Alexander Taylor

Alexander Taylor has given a whole new meaning to coat hangers and lampshades and his talent has not escaped the attention of Thorsten Van Elten, Established & Sons and Italian manufacturer Zanotta, not to mention *Elle Decoration*, which awarded Alexander 'Young Designer of the Year' in 2005 for his ingenious 'Antlers' coat hook.

## I. Simon Sankarayya, All of Us

BAFTA award-winner Simon Sankarayya, aka Sanky, hit us with a fast and funny journey thorough humorous images to provoke, surprise and re-contextualise. His images showed us how simplicity and pure thought can be the best way of getting a message across and how the world of design, ideas and observation can beat the tyranny of style hands down.

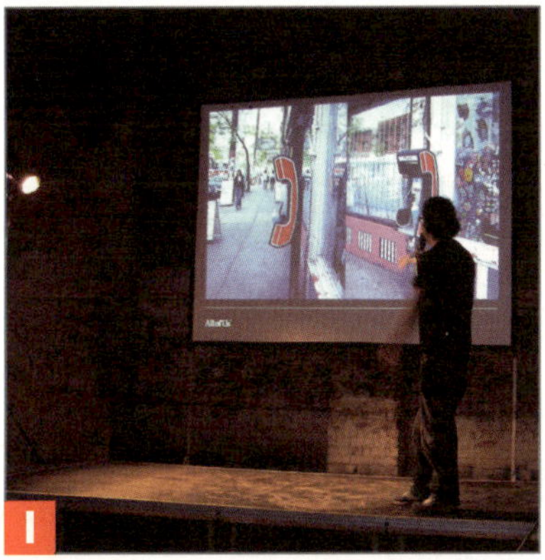


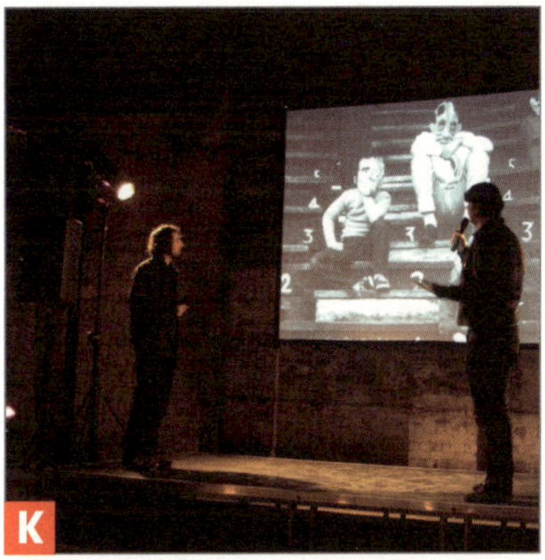


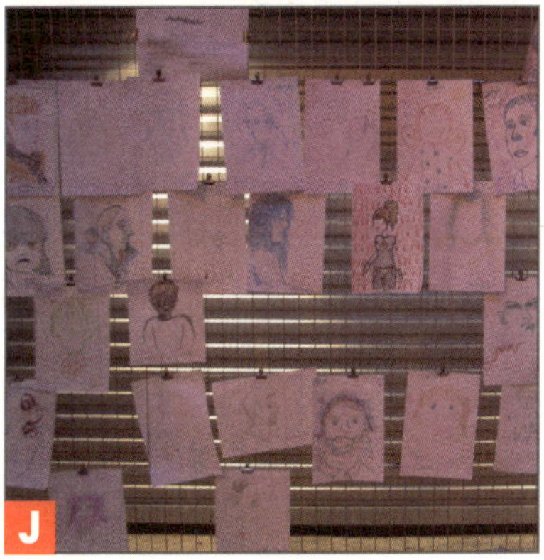


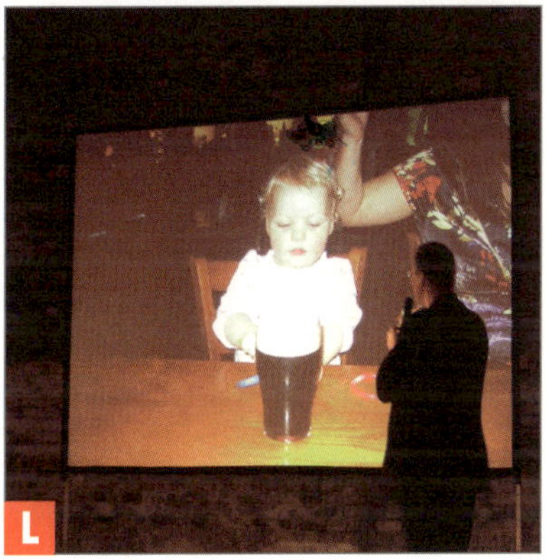


**I:** Simon Sankarayya, All of Us
**J:** at the break, audience members were asked to draw a picture of the person beside them. This is the gallery of portraits
**K:** Paul Read, Longest Mile Records and Ross Millard, Futureheads
**L:** Tim Bailey, xsite architecture

## K. Paul Read, Longest Mile Records and Ross Millard, Futureheads

Ross Millard established Longest Mile Records with close friend Paul Reed. He also plays guitar, writes and sings in the Futureheads. Ross and Paul immersed us in their world of duality, where the eternal search for that elusive musical genius continues…

## L. Tim Bailey, xsite Architecture

Tim Bailey, a man in pursuit of the perfect building project, shared images he loved from a world where all sorts of dualities exist. The image shows what Tim considers to be the most enduring and most believed brand identity – 'Guinness is good for you!'

# Who's who

**Design Council and One NorthEast funded all projects**

**Dott 07 Projects:**

**Alzheimer100**
Alzheimer's Society (regional branches)
Centre of Excellence for Life Sciences (CELS)
Equal Arts
Institute for Ageing and Health
Newcastle General Hospital
Newcastle University
Professor Jim Edwardson
Dr Louise Robinson
South of Tyne and Wearside Mental Health NHS Trust
Tees & North East Yorkshire NHS Trust
The SMART Team
thinkpublic – Ian Drysdale, Ivo Gormley, Deborah Szebeko (Senior Producer)
Time Bank
Wolfson Research Centre

**D&AD**

**D&AD and winners**
**First**
Daniel Foster-Smith (Northumbria University)
**Second**
Wesley Richardson (Ravensbourne College of Design & Communication)
**Commendation**
James Godwin (Central Saint Martins College of Art and Design)
John Hudson (Staffordshire University)
Mark Nicoll (Middlesex University)

**Design and Sexual Health**
Centre for Design Research at Northumbria University
Centre for Sexual Health Research, Southampton University
Department of Health
Design and Sexual Health
Design Options – Gwendolyn Brandon, Louise Hulton (Senior Producer), Ben Singleton, Jenna Singleton
FPA
Gateshead Primary Care Trust
Government Office North East
Newcastle Primary Care Trust
North East Strategic Health Authority
Pasante
Jennie Winhall

**Design Event 07**
Arts Council
DE07: Karen Stone (Curator), Danielle Pender (Co-curator) and Kala Preston
Formica
NESTA
NewcastleGateshead Initiative
Danielle Pender
**Exhibition curators:**
alt gallery
Blanka
Bowes Museum
Candy
Cohda Design
Deadgood Ltd
Designed and Made
Globe City
ie
If You Could
Inspire
Lobster Foundation
National Glass Centre
Northern Architecture
Northern Gallery for Contemporary Art
Platform Projects
[re]design
Reg Vardy Gallery
Reluctant Hero
Sunderland University
Tyne and Wear Museums

**Eco Design Challenge**
Cohda Design - Richard Liddle
Enigma Interactive
Rachel Deller
Nick Devitt (Senior Producer)
NE6 Design Consultants
NESTA
Newcastle College – Phil Bawden
Martin Selman
The Edinburgh Centre for Carbon Management – Jill Burnett
Terra Infirma – Gareth Kane
**Designers into Schools:**
ade a studio – Ade Armstrong Purves
Arup – Carol Clarke, Lean Doody
Ash LLP – Michael Atkinson
C2M(UK) Ltd – Leon Tighe, Gary Thompson
Conran and Partners – Sebastian Conran
Corporate Element – Mark Pattinson
Design Council – Clare Brass
Design Options – Jenna Singleton

Jane Darbyshire & David Kendall Ltd – Stuart Franklin, Nicola Watson
Mushroom Works – Nick James
NE6 Design Consultants Ltd – David Coates
Newcastle University – Alex Reeves
Red Square Design – Paul Rea
Gillian Sanderson
Sustainable Development Commission – Sarah Bray, Lizzie Chatterjee
The Centre for Design Research – (Dr) Kevin Hilton
University of Lincoln – Thom Shardlow
XORdesign LTd – Marta Fores
xsite architecture – Tim Bailey
zero-waste design – Roy Shearer

**Low Carb Lane**
Ashington Credit Union
East Ashington Development Trust
East Ashington LIFE Initiative
Live | work – Ben Reason (Senior Producer), Murray Sim, Alex Webb Allen
npower
New and Renewable Energy Centre
National Energy Action
Northumberland Warm Zones Ltd
Wansbeck Local Strategic Partnership

**Mapping the Necklace**
Cornerstone Strategies – Beth Davidson, Susan Williamson (Senior Producer)
Durham 2020 Vision
NewcastleGateshead Initiative
Sony
The Durham Necklace Park
Venue Solutions

**Move Me**
Arriva
Berwick Community Centre
live | work – David Townson (Senior Producer), Natalie McGhee, Richard Telford
Northumbria City Council
Scremerston Community
Staff, parents and students of Scremerston First School
Sure Start

**New Work**
B Group
Bright Creatives
Enabling Concepts – Helen Kerrigan, Nathan Pellow (Senior Producer)
Fabriam Networks
Geko Landscapes
Lexica Communications
live | work
Nimis
Rozmic
The Highfield Wellness Centre
Whiptail Cycles

**Our Cyborg Future?**
Centre for Life – Ian Simmons
Curator: Andrew Caleya Chetty (Senior Producer)
Co-curator: Sabine Seymour
Tyne and Wear Museums
Land Design Studio Ltd
Learning Programme – students and staff at St Benet Biscop Catholic High School and at Durham Gilesgate Sports College
Lighting: David Atkinson Lighting Design
Logistics: Claire London and Simon MacColl
Outreach Programme – students and staff at the University of Northumbria
Members of Sight Service and North Tyneside Youth Service
Professional placements: Policy, Ethics and Life Sciences Research Centre (PEALS); Elio Caccavale – Institute for Human Genetics at the University of Newcastle; Francesca Steele – Embryo Human Development Resource; Jayne Wallis – Institute of Ageing and Health at the University of Newcastle
NewcastleGateshead Initiative
Soundtrack: Steve Jones and Sally Rodgers
Videos: Studio Simple and Tribeat
Writers: David Bergin and Marie O'Mahony

**OurNewSchool**
Co-design team – Mike Collier, Kath Davidson, Steve Gater
Engine – Joe Heapy (Senior Producer), Steve Lee, Julia Schaeper
Walker Technology College

**Picture House, Film, Art and Design at Belsay**
Arts Council
Commissioned artists: Golan Levin, Bengt Sjolen, Adam Somlai-Fischer, United Visual Artists
Curator: Judith King

Dott 07 Curator: Juha Huuskonen
English Heritage
Esmee Fairbairn Foundation
Heritage Lottery Fund
Northern Rock Foundation
Northumberland Strategic
Partnership

**RSA Design Directions**
Ann Crawley
Janet Hawken
Susan Hewer

**RSA Design Direction Winners**
Konstantinos Chalaris
Lorna Cochrane
Dawn Danby
Lucy Denham
Linzi Deprez
Jotis Moore
Wesley Richardson
Mary Rick
Jyoti Stephens
Lisa Stockton

**Sustainable Tourism – Design Camp**
Amec Wind
Fawside Trust
Helen Jamieson
Steve Messam (Senior Producer)
Natural England
Ouseburn Trust
Cecilia Stenbom
**Camp Teams:**
PBPower
Guy Schofield (animation)
**Allendale**
Allendale Estates
Monica Chong
English Heritage
Environment Agency
Island6 Arts Center
Project It (campervan installation)
James Rokos
Vincenzon di Maria
Christina Worsing
**Team Wind**
Amanda Lwin
Annabel Bradbury
Fold
Justin Johnson
Konstantinos Chalaris
Mike Thompson
Stephanie Chen
**Urban Camping**
Martin Beyerle
Celine Dalcher
Linzi Rachel Deprez
Lorna Murray Cochrane
Patrick Quinn
**Design Camp Mentors:**
Beth Davidson
Beckie Dodds
Mikael Genberg
Antonio Izzo
Leandro Pisano

**Urban Farming**
David Barrie (Senior Producer)
Bioregional Quintain Ltd
bohn & viljoen architects – Andre Viljoen and Katrin Bohn
Connexions
Groundwork South Tees
Middlesbrough Council – Ian Collingwood
Middlesbrough Environment City
Middlesbrough Institute of Modern Art
Middlesbrough Partnership
Middlesbrough Primary Care Trust (PCT)
Middlesbrough Town Centre Company
Northern Rock Foundation
One NorthEast
Debra Solomon (Culiblog.org)
Stronger Together East Middlesbrough
The North East Regional Food Group
Tubbyphunk – Robert Page
Zest Innovation – Nina Belk

**Welcomes**
Clarences Community Centre
Clarences Community Farm
Marcus Coates
Huw Davies
Durham Tees Valley Airport
Erimus Housing
Film and Media Arts Festival
Football First (Middlesbrough Football Club in the Community)
Hemlington Community Cafe
High Clarence Community School
Media 19 – Nick Oldham, Belinda Williams
Middlesbrough Art Development Team
NewcastleGateshead Initiative – David Bilton, Stella Hall (Senior Producer)
Middlesbrough Central Library

**Vital Signs: Town Crying**
Arts Council
Forma (Senior Producer)
Lone Twin
NewcastleGateshead Initiative

**Vital Signs: Landscape/Portrait**
Artist: Kevin Carter
Arts Council
Babel Digital
d|lab
Data supplied by: upmystreet.com
Digital City
Digital Knowledge
Exchange
Fluid Pixels Studio
Forma (Senior Producer)
Media 19
NewcastleGateshead Initiative
University Teesside

**Creative Community Award Judges**
Claire Byers
Holly Francomb
Vikas Kumar
Max Lamb
Paul Younger

**Dott 07 Board**
Alan Clarke
Penny Egan
Jackie Fisher
David Kester
Chris Thompson

**Dott 07 Core Team**
Susan Ambrosi
Katherine Bain
Claire Capaldi
Beckie Darlington
Nick Devitt
Louise Fowler (Design Council)
Stacy Hall (One NorthEast)
Ruth Hasnip (Design Council)
Caitlin Hood
Cara Bell-Jones
Susan Lowthian
Emer McCourt
Stephen Moretti
Jonathan Neal (One NorthEast)
Robert O'Dowd
Georgia Rakusen
Lynsey Robinson (One NorthEast)
John Thackara
Adam Thomas
Jo Wilson

**Dott 07 Festival architects**
xsite - Tim Bailey, Nicola Gartland, Christoph Oschatz

**Intersections 07**
Kevin McCullagh
Northumbria University School of Design

**Photographers**
Phyllis Christopher
Andy Taylor

**Companies that worked with Dott 07**
BALTIC Centre for Contemporary Art
Bibliotheque
Blue River
Circus
Cool Blue
Different
Exposure
Gateshead Council
Groundwork South Tyneside and Newcastle
Infratech - Ian Fraser
Karen Morris
Kit Grover
NE6 Design Consultants Ltd
Origins
Press Ahead
Robin Mackie
Sony
The Crack – Mandy Baxter and Joe White
The National Glass Centre
Wardour – Molly Bennett, Simoney Girard, Rob Loveday, Linda Ososami, Alex Perchard, Barney Pickard
Warm Design
Will Wiles

**Doors of Perception**
Programme Director – John Thackara
The Doors team

# Partners and stakeholders

Design Council

one NorthEast
Regional Development Agency

world-class culture

north east england

Alzheimer's Society
Leading the fight against dementia

thinkpublic

TYNE & WEAR museums

ARTS COUNCIL ENGLAND

designoptions
information and design for better services

DE07
design event

The Centre for Design Research

Life

Gateshead NHS
Primary Care Trust

Pasante healthcare

NESTA
Making Innovation Flourish

supporting rural contemporary art

FORMICA

live|work

Middlesbrough
moving forward

D&AD
For Excellence
For Education
For Enterprise
and not for profit

xsite

the DigitalCity
creativity, imagination and daring

UpMyStreet

UNIVERSITY OF TEESSIDE

NaREC

NSP
Northumberland Strategic Partnership

TimeBank

East Ashington Life
Local initiative for everyone

npower

NORTHUMBERLAND
COUNTY COUNCIL

NEA
Campaigning for Warm Homes

warm zone
working together for warm homes
in Northumberland

Bright

cornerstone

enabling concepts

NaREC

SureStart

SONY

2020VISION
DURHAM CITY CENTRE

Lexica
COMMUNICATIONS

thebgroup

East Ashington
Development Trust

fabriam
NETWORKS

northern rock
foundation

ARRIVA

Rozmic

www.forma.org.uk

media 19

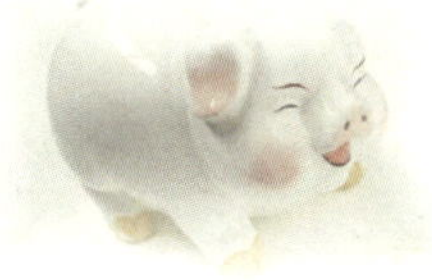

RSA

Engine

nimis
LIMITED

whiptail
CYCLES

SCREMERSTON
First School

ENGLISH HERITAGE

venuesolutions

Middlesbrough
Primary Care Trust

NHS

culiblog.org

Zest
innovation

BioRegional

QUINTAIN
ESTATES AND DEVELOPMENT PLC

# References


**1.** Indicators of climate change in the UK
www.ecn.ac.uk/iccuk/

**2.** *Natural Capitalism*, Paul Hawken, Amory Lovins and Hunter Lovins, London: Earthscan (1999)

**3.** *Natural Capitalism*, Paul Hawken, Amory Lovins and Hunter Lovins, London: Earthscan (1999)

**4.** New Mobility Agenda
www.ecoplan.org/wtpp/wt_index.htm

**5.** New Mobility Agenda
www.ecoplan.org/wtpp/wt_index.htm

**6.** Widex Noise Report: *Traffic Noise in England* (2007), Deepak Prasher, Professor of Audiology, The Ear Institute University College London

**7.** *Is man the only cause of climate change?* Jean-Marc Jancovici, www.manicore.com/anglais/documentation _a/greenhouse/only_action.html

**8.** Sector Skills Agreement, North East England (January 2007) www.lantra.co.uk/documents/NESSAStage5.pdf

**9.** *The way to work in 2016*, Orange (2007)
www.business.orange.co.uk/servlet/Satellite?pagename=Business&c=OUKPage&cid=1044133326057

**10.** 2007 City & Guilds Happiness Index
www.city-and-guilds.co.uk/cps/rde/xchg/SID-0AC0478D-E8BF11C0/cgonline/hs.xsl/2342.html

**11.** Design Council www.designcouncil.info/futurecurrents/HM_energy_statement.php

**12.** Danish Board of District Heating
www.dbdh.dk/dkmap/dkmap.html

**13.** Sustainable Schools
www.teachernet.gov.uk/sustainableschools

**14.** 'Deschooling society', Ivan Illich, (*World perspectives*, v. 44) Harper & Row (1971)

**15.** *Learning beyond the classroom: education for a changing world*, Tom Bentley, Routledge Demos (1998)

**16.** *Improving the health of the world's poorest people*, Population Reference Bureau
www.prb.org/pdf04/ImprovingtheHealthbrief_Eng.pdf

**17.** World Health Organisation
www.who.int/whosis/indicators/2007LEX0/en/index.html

**18.** Profile of Informal and Family Caregivers, Bohse & Associates
www.bohse.com/html/facts_on_aging.html

**19.** Alzheimer's Society www.alzheimers.org.uk

**20.** Equality Strategy, Kent County Council
www.kent.gov.uk

**21.** http://en.wikipedia.org/wiki/Teenage_pregnancy

**22.** Toronto Food Policy Council
www.toronto.ca/health/tfpc_index.htm

**23.** *The Party's Over*, Richard Heinberg, New Society Publishers (2003), Gabriola Island, BC Canada
www.newsociety.com

**24.** Ecological debt – external debt
www.cosmovisiones.com/DeudaEcologica/a_alier01in.html

**25.** Toronto Food Policy Council
www.toronto.ca/health/tfpc_index.htm

**26.** Why Our Food is So Dependent on Oil, Norman Church, *Energy Bulletin* (2005)
www.energybulletin.net/5045.html

**27.** Eating Oil
www.resurgence.org/resurgence/issues/jones216.htm